TRAVELLING
THE PATH
OF LOVE

SAYINGS OF
SUFI MASTERS

EDITED BY
LLEWELLYN VAUGHAN-LEE

BIOGRAPHICAL NOTES BY
SARA SVIRI

First published in the United States in 1995 by
The Golden Sufi Center
P.O. Box 428, Inverness, California 94937

Second printing, 1995

Cover Design by Tennessee Dixon.
Printed and Bound by McNaughton & Gunn,
using recycled paper.

Library of Congress Cataloging in Publication Data,
Vaughan-Lee, Llewellyn
Travelling the Path of Love:
Sayings of Sufi Masters
1. Spirituality
2. Sufism
3. Poetry

Library of Congress Catalog Card Number: 94-078690
ISBN 0-9634574-2-X

CONTENTS

And we are guided by their footprints.

Qur'ān

INTRODUCTION

Sufism is a mystical path of love. It emerged in the Muslim world in the eighth century in small groups of seekers who were known as "Wayfarers on the Mystical Path." In their deep passion and longing for God they realized Truth as "The Beloved," and therefore also became known as "The Lovers of God." Later they were called Sufis, possibly referring to their white woolen garments (*Sûf*), or as an indication of their purity of heart (*Safâ'*). These small groups gathered around spiritual teachers and, in time, matured into fraternities and orders, with each order bearing the name of its initiator.

The essence of the Sufi path is the particular tradition passed down from teacher to disciple in an uninterrupted chain of transmission. Each Sufi order and teacher has certain practices and principles to help the wayfarer on the journey, to keep the fire of longing burning within the heart and the attention focused on the goal. The sayings and writings about the path help the wayfarer to develop the right attitude and qualities, and also to understand inner happenings that are often bewildering and confusing. The ways of love are very different from those of the mind.

The Sufi path has as its goal the state of union with God. For each traveller the journey to this goal is unique; it is the journey "of the alone to the Alone." Yet there are also stages which all seekers pass through, trials, processes of purification and transformation. It is these stages that the Sufi masters, or sheikhs, have attempted to describe. As guides they have mapped out the path of the heart and the mystical states that are experienced along the way.

The teachings and writings of the Sufis describe the soul's journey from separation to union with God. With the passion and depth of feeling that belong to lovers they outline the stages of this journey and give advice to other travellers. Sufi literature offers us the richest and most detailed understanding of the relationship of lover and Beloved, a relationship that is at the core of every mystical path.

Drawing on their own experiences, the Sufi masters describe the inner workings of the path of love. They tell how longing for God burns away our impurities.

They remind us that by remembering God we come closer to our eternal essence and that in our moments of utmost despair the Beloved reveals Himself: He who had seemed so distant is discovered "closer to you than yourself to yourself." They share their glimpses of the essential oneness of all life and, with simplicity, directness, and humor, describe the paradoxical nature of this mystical journey.

The ninth-century ecstatic Bâyezîd Bistâmî, who left no writings, is known for his utterances made in a state of divine intoxication, like "Glory be to me. How great is my majesty!" Al-Junayd, who taught in Baghdad in the ninth century, advocated a path of sobriety and the integration of mysticism into ordinary life. At the same time in Baghdad the prince of lovers, al-Hallâj, spoke of the essential unity of lover and Beloved and was put to death for exclaiming the mystical truth "*anâ'l-Haqq*" (I am the Absolute Truth). In the eleventh century in Nishapur the great master Abû Sa'îd ibn Abî-l-Khayr stressed the need to abandon the ego, or *nafs*, in order to realize the Pure Self.

These early mystics spoke a direct and simple language different from the more learned and scholarly writings of some of the later Sufis, as, for example, al-Ghazzâlî, who in the late eleventh century worked to reconcile the teachings of Islam, the "*sharî'a*," with the mystical path, the "*tarîqa*." A century later ibn 'Arabî, called "the greatest sheikh," and considered by many to be the greatest Muslim exponent of metaphysical doctrine, stressed the existence of One God and the Unity of Being (*wahdat al-wujûd*). A few years after ibn 'Arabî's death Jalâluddin Rûmî, spiritually awakened by his meeting with the wandering mystic Shams-i Tabrîz, began reciting one of the greatest mystical writings of all time, the *Mathnawî*, a treasure-house of spiritual lore.

Rûmî is the most widely read of the Sufi writers, and the contemporary translations of his work have made Sufism more known in the West. But he is only one of the many Sufis who, from the eighth century to the present day, have spoken and written about the path of love, of the pain and the bliss of the heart's opening to God. Each Sufi master is influenced by those who have gone before him, by the history of the tradition. But more important are the mystic's own experiences, his individual communion with the Beloved. This is the truth that speaks through their words, whether the direct utterances of the drunken Bâyezid Bistâmî, or the metaphysical work of ibn 'Arabî.

Language and culture may change with time and place, but the inner workings of the heart remain the same. The essence of the mystical quest is beyond time and space, beyond all form. What the Sufi masters say about love speaks to all who long for their Real Home. They help to remind us of our divine nature and provide signposts on the way back to our innermost self. These lovers of God speak the direct language of spiritual experience, language that carries the conviction of those who have tasted Truth.

This selection of Sufi sayings is offered as inspiration for fellow-travellers on whatever path they may be following. The Sufi says that there are as many ways to God as there are human beings, "as many as the breaths of the children of God." Within each of us there is the call to "open your hidden eyes and come, return to the root of the root of your own self." This journey of the soul is mankind's most primal dream. It is the deepest purpose of life. On this journey we are in the company of all those who have gone before us. *We are guided by their footprints.*

LLEWELLYN VAUGHAN-LEE, EDITOR

THE SUFI

Sufism is defined as "truth with-out form," and the Sufi aspires to become "featureless and formless," to be so lost in God that only He remains. But there are certain qualities that belong to these travellers on the path of love.

The Sufis are folk who have preferred God to everything, so that God has preferred them to everything.

DHÛ-L-NÛN

The Sufi is he who aims, from at first, at reaching God, the Creative Truth. Until he has found what he seeks, he takes no rest, nor does he give heed to any person. For Thy sake I haste over land and water; over the plain I pass and the mountain I cleave and from everything I turn my face, until the time when I reach that place where I am alone with Thee.

AL-HALLÂJ

To be a Sufi is to give up all worries and there is no worse worry than yourself. When you are occupied with self you are separated from God. The way to God is but one step: the step out of yourself.

ABÛ SA'ÎD IBN ABÎ-L-KHAYR

The Sufi is absent from himself and present with God.

HUJWÎRÎ

A Sufi is a day that needs no sun, a night that needs no moon or star, and a non-being that needs no being.

ABÛ'L-HASAN 'ALI AL-KHARAQÂNÎ

Sufism means that God causes you to die to yourself and gives you life in Him.

AL-JUNAYD

The Sufi is separated from mankind and united with God, as God has said, "And I chose thee for Myself," that is, He separated him from all others.

AL-SHÎBLÎ

To be a Sufi means to abide continuously with God and to be at peace with men.

AL-GHAZZÂLÎ

The Sufi is pleased with all that God does in order that God may be pleased with all that he does.

ABÛ SAʿÎD IBN ABÎ-L-KHAYR

Sufism is that the servant acts according to whatever is most fitting to the moment.

ʿAMR IBN ʿUTHMÂN AL-MAKKÎ

When al-Junayd was asked about the mystic, he replied, "The color of water is the color of its container. That is, the nature of the mystic is always determined by the nature of his state at a given moment."

AL-JUNAYD

5

One of the attributes of the saint[1] is that he has no fear, for fear is anticipating some disagreeable event that might come or expecting that something beloved might pass away in the future. The saint is concerned only with the present moment. He has no future to fear.

TRADITIONAL

The Sufi is like the earth, on which every foul thing is thrown and from which fair things come forth.

AL-JUNAYD

---

[1] In Sufism a saint, *Walī*, is a "friend of God," someone who is under the special protection of God.

A man will not be a mystic until he is like the earth—both the righteous and the sinner tread upon it—and until he is like the clouds—they shade all things—and until he is like the rain—it waters all things, whether it loves them or not.

BÂYEZÎD BISTÂMÎ

When Abû Saʿîd ibn Abî-l-Khayr was asked what Sufism entailed he replied: "Whatever you have in your mind—forget it; whatever you have in your hand—give it; whatever is to be your fate—face it!"

ABÛ SAʿÎD IBN ABÎ-L-KHAYR

The Sufi is he to whom nothing is attached, and who does not become attached to anything.

NÛRÎ

Be in this world as if you are a traveller, a passer-by, with your clothes and shoes full of dust. Sometimes you sit under the shade of a tree, sometimes you walk in the desert. Be always a passer-by, for this is not home.

HADÎTH

"Dervishes" [2] is a term which refers to holy poverty: "the poor man is not he whose hand is empty of provisions, but he whose nature is empty of desires."

HUJWÎRÎ

---

[2] Dervish is a Persian term referring to a state of spiritual poverty. The early dervishes were wandering ascetics.

A dervish wearing a sackcloth coat and woolen cap once came to meet Master Abû ʿAlî. One of Abû ʿAlî's disciples tried to humor him, saying, "How much did you purchase that sackcloth for?"

The dervish answered, "I purchased it for the sum of the world. I was offered the hereafter in exchange, but refused to trade."

Abû ʿAlî ad-Daqqâq

Sufism means that you possess nothing and nothing possesses you.

Sumnûn

Only the bondsmen are free!

Hâfiz

The Sufi is he that keeps a pure heart towards God.

BISHR IBN AL-HÂRITH AL-HÂFÎ

You are a Sufi when your heart is as soft and as warm as wool.

TRADITIONAL

Sufism is staying at the lover's door even when you are driven away.

RÛDHBÂRÎ

Dervishes are a brotherhood of migrants who keep watch on the world and for the world.

ANONYMOUS

Four thousand years before God created these bodies, He created the souls and kept them beside Himself and shed a light upon them. He knew what quantity each soul received and He showed favor to each in proportion to its illumination. The souls remained all that time in light, until they became fully nourished. Those who in this world live in joy and agreement with one another must have been akin to one another in that place. Here they love one another and are called the friends of God, and they are brothers who love one another for God's sake. These souls know one another by smell, like horses.

ABÛ SA'ÎD IBN ABÎ-L-KHAYR

If you keep the company of the truthful, be truthful with them, for they are spies of the hearts. They come into your hearts and leave without your becoming aware.

AHMAD B. ʿASIM AL-ANTÂKÎ

God speaks out of the innermost being of the mystic while he is silent.

AL-JUNAYD

Sufism is not preached, and it is even taught in some cases by example and guidance which may be unknown to the learner's ordinary faculties.

ANONYMOUS

The Sufi bows down before none but God.

TRADITIONAL

There was a king, who, one day, entering his royal court, observed one person who among all those present, was not bowing down before him. Unnerved by the impudent act of this stranger in the hall, the king called out: "How dare you not bow down before me! Only God does not bow down before me, and there is nothing greater than God. Who then are you?" The tattered stranger answered with a smile, "I am that nothing."

ANONYMOUS

The true Sufi is he that is nothing.

TRADITIONAL

THE PATH

The mystical path is the soul's journey from separation back to union. On this homeward journey we are seeking our own innermost essence, the pearl of great price that lies hidden within the heart.

The Sufi travels three Journeys—the Journey from God, the Journey to God, and the Journey in God.

TRADITIONAL

Your journey is towards your homeland. Remember you are travelling from the world of appearances to the world of Reality.

'ABD'L-KHÂLIQ GHIJDUWÂNÎ

No one by himself
    can find the Path to Him
Whoever goes to His street
    goes with His feet.

MAGHRIBÎ

If you walk toward Him, He comes to you running.

Hadîth

The first step is to cease isolating oneself from God.

al-Hallâj

You too put your best foot forward. If you do not wish to, then follow your fantasies. But if you prefer the secrets of the love of your soul you will sacrifice everything. You will lose what you consider valuable, but you will soon hear the sacramental word "Enter."

'Attâr

An intending disciple said to Dhû-l-Nûn, the Egyptian: "Above everything in this world I wish to enroll in the Path of Truth."

Dhû-l-Nûn told him: "You can accompany our caravan only if you first accept two things. One is that you will have to do things which you do not want to do. The other is that you will not be permitted to do things which you desire to do. It is 'wanting' which stands between man and the Path of Truth."

DHÛ-L-NÛN

Take one step
        away from yourself and—
                behold!—the Path!

ABÛ SA'ÎD IBN ABÎ-L-KHAYR

Know that when you learn to lose yourself, you will reach the Beloved. There is no other secret to be learnt, and more than that is not known to me.

AL-ANSÂRÎ

A man came to Abû 'Alî ad-Daqqâq and said, "I have come to you from a very distant place."

Abû 'Alî ad-Daqqâq replied, "Attaining knowledge of the path has nothing to do with traversing great distances and undergoing journeys. Separate from yourself even by one single step, and your goal will be reached."

Abû 'Alî ad-Daqqâq

I saw my Lord in my dreams and I asked, "How am I to find You?" He replied, "Leave yourself and come!"

Bâyezîd Bistâmî

He travels with whoever looks for Him, and having taken the seeker by the hand, He arouses him to go in search of himself.

al-Ansârî

In your own land seek the hidden flame.... It is unworthy of man to borrow light from elsewhere.

AL-HALLÂJ

If you are man enough for this path you must take your heart in hand. That, so the specialists say, is the only work worthy of the name.

JÂMÎ

When you seek God, seek Him in your heart—
He is not in Jerusalem, nor in Mecca nor in the *hajj*.

YÛNUS EMRE

The minute I heard my first love story
I started looking for you
Not knowing how blind I was.

Lovers don't finally meet somewhere.
They're in each other all along.

RÛMÎ

When truth has taken hold of a heart she empties it of
all but Herself.

AL-HALLÂJ

God is jealous, and one sign of His jealousy is that
He does not clear any way through to Himself other
than Himself.

AL-HALLÂJ

Abu'l Hasan Pusanji was asked, "What is faith and what is trust in God?"

He replied: "You eat what is in front of you and chew each mouthful well with a tranquil heart, knowing that whatever belongs to you, you will not lose."

ABU'L HASAN PUSANJI

One day a man from Mount Locam came to visit Sarî al-Saqatî.

"Sheikh So-and-So from Mount Locam greets you," he said.

"He dwells in the mountains," commented Sarî. "So his efforts amount to nothing. A man ought to be able to live in the midst of the market and be so preoccupied with God that not for a single minute is he absent from God."

SARÎ

Our way is that of group discussion. In solitude there is renown and in renown there is peril. Welfare is to be found in a group. Those who follow this way find great benefit and blessing in group meetings.

Bahâ ad-dîn Naqshband

The perfect mystic is not an ecstatic devotee lost in contemplation of Oneness, nor a saintly recluse shunning all commerce with mankind, but "the true saint" goes in and out amongst the people and eats and sleeps with them and buys and sells in the market and marries and takes part in social intercourse, and never forgets God for a single moment.

Abû Sa'îd ibn Abî-l-Khayr

First tie your camel's knee and then trust in God.

HADÎTH

Wear with mankind what they wear and eat what they
eat. But be separate from them inwardly.

ABÛ 'ALÎ AD-DAQQÂQ

Solitude in the crowd: in all your outward activity
remain inwardly free. Learn not to identify with anything
whatsoever.

'ABD'L-KHÂLIQ GHIJDUWÂNÎ

Opportunity is precious and time is a sword.

Saʿdî

If all you have is a few copper coins in one pocket, those coins are of great value to you. But if someone places a thousand gold pieces in your other pocket, those few copper coins are no longer important.

Anonymous

To meet You I look at face after face, appearance after appearance.... To see Your face I pass by like the morning wind.

al-Hallâj

Shiblî sought Junayd as a teacher and said to him, "You are recommended as an expert on pearls (enlightenment and wisdom).... Either give me one, or sell one to me."

"If I sell you one, you will not have the price of it, and if I give you one, having so easily come by it you will not realize its value," Junayd replied. "Do like me; plunge head-first into this Sea, and if you wait patiently you will obtain your pearl."

AL-JUNAYD

Search, no matter what situation you are in.
O thirsty one, search for water constantly.
Finally, the time will come when you will reach
   the spring.

RÛMÎ

It is a grave error for anyone to imagine he will attain anything or that anything will be revealed to him of the Path without persistent striving on his part.

Abû 'Uthmân al-Hîrî

The thing we tell of can never be found by seeking, yet only seekers find it.

Bâyezîd Bistâmî

Whoever believes he can reach God by his own efforts
toils in vain; whoever believes he can reach God without
effort is merely a traveller on the road of intent.

ABÛ SA'ÎD AL-KHARRÂZ

When you think you have found Him, that very instant
you have lost Him. And when you think you have lost
Him, then you have found Him.

ABÛ SA'ÎD IBN ABÎ-L-KHAYR

And if He closes before you all the ways and passes,
He will show you a hidden way which nobody knows.

RÛMÎ

Keep strenuously toiling along this path,
Do not rest until the last breath; for
That last breath may yet bring the blessings
    from the Knower of all things.

Rûmî

No one learned the art of archery from Me
Who did not make Me, in the end, the target.

Sa'dî

Like the hunter, the Sufi chases game; he sees the tracks
    left by the musk deer and follows them.
For a while it is the tracks which are his clues, but later
    it is the musk itself which guides him.

Rûmî

A path and a gateway have no meaning once the
objective is in sight.

HUJWÎRÎ

Everything in the world of existence has an end and a
goal. The end is maturity and the goal is freedom. For
example, fruit grows on the tree until it is ripe and then
falls. The ripened fruit represents maturity, and the fallen
fruit, freedom.

The final goal is returning to one's origin. Everything
which reaches its origin has reached its goal. A farmer
sows grain in the ground and tends it. It begins to grow,
eventually seeds, and again becomes grain. It has returned
to its original form. The circle is complete. Completing
the circle of existence is freedom.

NASAFÎ

The inner pilgrim wraps himself in the light of the holy spirit, transforming his material shape into the inner essence, and circumambulating the shrine of the heart, inwardly reciting the name of God. He moves in circles because the path of the essence is not straight but circular. Its end is its beginning.

'Abdu'l-Qâdir al-Gîlânî

Dhû-l-Nûn was asked, "What is the end of the mystic?"
He answered, "When he is as he was where he was before he was."

Dhû-l-Nûn

THE TEACHER AND THE DISCIPLE

The Sufis say that you need a teacher as a guide on the mystical path. The teacher is someone who is surrendered to God and is able to help the wayfarer make the transition from the ego to the Self. In surrendering to the teacher, fanâ fî'l Sheikh, *the disciple learns to surrender to God,* fanâ fî'llâh.

In the beginning you must do two things. One is journeying and the other is you must take a master.

ABÛ'L-HASAN 'ALÎ AL-KHARAQÂNÎ

Choose a master, for without him this journey is full of tribulations, fears, and dangers. With no escort, you would be lost on a road you would have already taken. Do not travel alone on the Path.

RÛMÎ

It is easier to drag along a mountain by a hair than to emerge from the self by oneself.

ABÛ SA'ÎD IBN ABÎ-L-KHAYR

Do not take a step
on the path of love without a guide.
I have tried it
one hundred times and failed.

HÂFIZ

Abû Sa'îd was asked, "If someone wishes, is it possible to travel the mystic path without a teacher?"

The Sheikh replied, "It is impossible because someone is required to guide him along the way, someone who has already reached the goal travelling that path, who will tell him what are faults and what are virtues on this path. At each stage he will say this is the such-and-such stage, here one must remain a little longer. And if there is a dangerous place somewhere, he will tell him to be on his guard, and will give him kindly encouragement, so that travelling that path with a strengthened heart, he may reach the goal.

"When he has reached the goal he will find peace."

ABÛ SA'ÎD IBN ABÎ-L-KHAYR

Whoever travels without a guide
needs two hundred years for a two-days' journey.

RÛMÎ

The moment you are united with the master, it
becomes effortless.

BHAI SAHIB

Then there arises the question of how to find the real guru. Very often people are in doubt, they do not know whether the guru they see is a true or false guru. Frequently a person comes in contact with a false guru in a world where there is so much falsehood. But at the same time a real seeker, one who is not false to himself, will always meet with the truth, with the real, because it is his own real faith, his own sincerity in earnest seeking that will become his torch. The real teacher is within, the lover of reality is one's own sincere self, and if one is really seeking truth, sooner or later one will certainly find a true teacher. And supposing one came into contact with a false teacher, what then? Then the real One will turn the false teacher into a real teacher, because Reality is greater than falsehood.

INAYAT KHAN

People think that a Sheikh should show miracles and manifest illumination. The requirement of a teacher, however, is only that he should possess all that the disciple needs.

IBN ʿARABÎ

Abû Sa'îd was asked, "Who is the spiritual guide who has attained to Truth, and who is the sincere disciple?"

The Sheikh replied, "The spiritual guide who attained to Truth is he in whom at least ten characteristics are found, as proof of his authenticity:

First, he must have become a goal, to be able to have a disciple.

Second, he must have travelled the mystic path himself, to be able to show the way.

Third, he must have become refined and educated, to be able to be an educator.

Fourth, he must be generous and devoid of self-importance, so that he can sacrifice wealth on behalf of the disciple.

Fifth, he must have no hand in the disciple's wealth, so that he is not tempted to use it for himself.

Sixth, whenever he can give advice through a sign, he will not use direct expression.

Seventh, whenever he can educate through kindness, he will not use violence and harshness.

Eighth, whatever he orders, he has first accomplished himself.

Ninth, whatever he forbids the disciple, he has abstained from himself.

Tenth, he will not abandon for the world's sake the disciple he accepts for the sake of God.

If the spiritual guide is like this and is adorned with these character traits, the disciple is bound to be sincere and a good traveller, for what appears in the disciple is the quality of the spiritual guide made manifest in the disciple."

As for the sincere disciple, the Sheikh has said, "No less than the ten characteristics which I mention must be present in the sincere disciple, if he is to be worthy of discipleship:

First, he must be intelligent enough to understand the spiritual guide's indications.

Second, he must be obedient in order to carry out the spiritual guide's command.

Third, he must be sharp of hearing to perceive what the spiritual guide says.

Fourth, he must have an enlightened heart in order to see the spiritual guide's greatness.

Fifth, he must be truthful, so that whatever he reports, he reports truthfully.

Sixth, he must be true to his word, so that whatever he says, he keeps his promise.

Seventh, he must be generous, so that whatever he has, he is able to give away.

Eighth, he must be discreet, so that he can keep a secret.

Ninth, he must be receptive to advice, so that he will accept the guide's admonition.

Tenth, he must be chivalrous in order to sacrifice his own dear life on the mystic path.

Having these character traits, the disciple will more easily accomplish his journey and more quickly reach the goal set for him on the mystic path by the spiritual guide."

ABÛ SA'ÎD IBN ABÎ-L-KHAYR

It should be borne in mind that the function of the disciple is to focus a stream of energy of some special kind upon the physical plane where it can become an attractive center of force and draw to itself similar types of ideas and thought currents, which are not strong enough to live by themselves or to make a sufficiently strong impact upon human consciousness.

IRINA TWEEDIE

Love cannot be more or less for the Teacher. For him the very beginning and the end are the same; it is a closed circle. His love for the disciple does not go on increasing; for the disciple, of course, it is very different; he has to complete the whole circle.... As the disciple progresses he feels the Master nearer and nearer, as the time goes on. But the Master is not nearer; he was always near, only the disciple did not know it.

BHAI SAHIB

God is nowhere. God can only be known through the Master. If you are being merged into the Teacher, you will know God. Only the Teacher is important for you. Only the Teacher. The Divine Master is complete in every way. By simply becoming like him one becomes complete in every way....

BHAI SAHIB

I am transcendent reality, and I am the tenuous thread that brings it very close. I am the secret of man in his very act of existing, and I am that invisible one who is the object of worship.... I am the Sheikh with the divine nature, and I am the guardian of the world of human nature.

JÎLÎ, ON KHIDR

The spiritual master is to his community, what the prophet is to his nation.

ABÛ SAʻÎD IBN ABÎ-L-KHAYR

Saints are like rivers, they flow where they are directed.... If a Hint is there, I have to do it, and if I don't, I am MADE to do it. A Divine Hint is an Order. Sometimes the Saints have to do things the people will misjudge, and which from the worldly point of view could be condemned, because the world judges by appearances. One important quality required on the Path is never to judge by appearances. More often than not things look different from what they really are. There is no good and evil for the Creator. Only human society makes it so. A Saint is beyond good and evil, but Saints are people of the highest morality and will never give a bad example.

BHAI SAHIB

The saint is a fragrant plant placed in the earth by God. The truthful take in his fragrance and it comes into their hearts so that they long for their Master. Then they increase their worship according to their different natures.

Yahyâ ibn Mu'âdh ar-Râzî

The saints of God are known by three signs: their thought is of God, their dwelling is in God, and their business is with God.

Ma'rûf al-Karkhî

O you who stab the selfless one with the sword, you are
    stabbing yourself with it. Beware!
For the selfless one has passed away, he has become a
    mirror:
    naught is there but the image of another's face.
If you spit at it, you spit at your own face; and if you
    strike the mirror,
    you strike yourself.
And if you see an ugly face in the mirror, 'tis you;
    and if you see Jesus and Mary, 'tis you.
He is neither this nor that: he is pure and free from self;
    he puts your image before you.

RŮMÎ

The Teacher is without a face and without a name.

TRADITIONAL

Last night my teacher taught me the lesson of Poverty:
Having nothing and wanting nothing.

Rûmî

We are the means of reaching the goal. It is necessary
that seekers should cut themselves away from us and think
only of the goal.

Bahâ ad-dîn Naqshband

The only guide to God is God Himself.

Kalâbâdhî

THE LONGING OF THE HEART

*The heart's longing for God is
the pain of separation. This primal
cry of the soul draws the lover
back to the arms of the Beloved.*

Listen to the reed how it tells a tale,
  complaining of separations,
Saying, "Ever since I was parted from the reed-bed,
  my lament has caused man and woman to moan.
It is only to a bosom torn by severance that I can unfold
  the pain of love-desire.
Everyone who is left far from his source wishes back
  the time when he was united with it."

RÛMÎ

The source of my grief and loneliness is deep in
  my breast.
This is a disease no doctor can cure.
Only union with the Friend can cure it.

RÂBI'A

I will cry to Thee and cry to Thee and cry to Thee
Until the milk of Thy kindness boils up.

RÛMÎ

If the eight Paradises were opened in my hut, and the
rule of both worlds were given in my hands, I would not
give for them that single sigh which rises at morning-time
from the depth of my soul in remembering my longing
for Him.

BÂYEZÎD BISTÂMÎ

Oh Lord, nourish me not with love but with the desire
for love.

IBN 'ARABÎ

Give me the pain of Love, the Pain of Love for Thee!
Not the joy of Love, just the Pain of Love,
And I will pay the price, any price you ask!
All myself I will offer for it, and the price you will ask
    on top of it!
Keep the joy for others, give me the Pain,
And gladly will I pay for the Pain of Love!

ANONYMOUS

Longing is a state of commotion in the heart hoping
for meeting with the Beloved. The depth of longing is
commensurate with the servant's love of God.

AL-QUSHAYRÎ

The world is full of beautiful things until an old man
with a beard came into my life and set my heart aflame
with longing and made it pregnant with love. How can
I look at the loveliness around me, how can I see it,
if it hides the face of my Lover?

PERSIAN SONG

A sweet smell has the dust at the feet of my Guru; never
I cried before, but now there is no end of sorrow for me....

TRADITIONAL

If God, when He created the world, had created no creatures in it; and if He had filled it full of millet from East to West and from earth to heaven; and if then He had created one bird and bidden it eat one grain of this millet every thousand years, and if, after that, He had created a man and kindled in his heart this mystic longing and had told him that he would never win to his goal until this bird left not a single millet-seed in the whole world, and that he would continue until then in this burning pain of love—I have been thinking, it would still be a thing soon ended!

ABÛ SAʿÎD IBN ABÎ-L-KHAYR

The inner truth of desire is that it is a restive motion in the heart in search of God.

AL-QUSHAYRÎ

There are those among you who desire this world and there are those among you who desire the world to come. But where is He who desires God?

AL-SHÎBLÎ

I am calling to you from afar;
Calling to you since the very beginning of days.
Calling to you across millennia,
For aeons of time—
Calling—calling.... Since always....
It is part of your being, my voice,
But it comes to you faintly and you only hear it sometimes;
"I don't know," you may say.
But somewhere you know.
"I can't hear," you say, "what is it and where?"
But somewhere you hear, and deep down you know.
For I am that in you which has been always;
I am that in you which will never end.
Even if you say, "Who is calling?"
Even if you think, "Who is that?"
Where will you run? Just tell me.
Can you run away from yourself?

For I am the Only One for you;
There is no other,
Your Promise, your Reward am I alone—
Your Punishment, your longing
And your Goal....

ANONYMOUS

Someone asked Râbi'a, "I have committed many sins; if I turn in penitence towards God, will He turn in mercy towards me?"

"Nay," she replied, "but if He shall turn towards thee, thou wilt turn towards Him."

RÂBI'A

Until the beam of His love shines out to guide the soul,
It does not set out to behold the love of His Face.
My heart feels not the slightest attraction towards Him
Until an attraction comes from Him and works upon my
    heart.
Since I learnt that He longs for me, longing for Him
    never leaves me for an instant.

MAGHRIBÎ

If the magnet were not loving, how could it attract
    the iron with such longing?
And if love were not there, the straw would not seek
    the amber.

Nizâmî

Not only the thirsty seek the water,
the water as well seeks the thirsty.

Rûmî

Spiritual need is a living and luminous fire placed by God in the breasts of His servants that their "self" (*nafs,* or ego) may be burned; and when it has been burned this fire becomes the fire of "longing" (*shawq*) which never dies, neither in this world nor in the next.

ABŪ SA'ĪD IBN ABĪ-L-KHAYR

One must have "spiritual need," for there is no shorter way to God for the devotee; if it passes through solid rock, water springs forth. "Spiritual need" is fundamental for the Sufis; it is the bestowal of God's mercy upon them.

ABŪ SA'ĪD IBN ABĪ-L-KHAYR

You'll be free from the trap of your being,
    when, through spiritual need,
You're trodden underfoot, like a mat,
    in the mosque and the winehouse.

SANÂ'Î

Ecstasy is a flame which springs up in the secret heart, and appears out of longing.

PAUL NWYIA

Open your hidden eyes and return to the root of the root of your own self.

RÛMÎ

When it is possible to hear the Beloved speak Himself,
why listen to second-hand reports?

JÂMÎ

Know that you are the veil which conceals yourself
from you. Know also that you cannot reach God through
yourself, but that you reach Him through Him. The reason
is that when God vouchsafes the vision of reaching Him,
He calls upon you to seek after Him and you do.

AL-JUNAYD

It is he who suffers his absence in me
Who through me cries out to himself.
Love's most strange, most holy mystery—
We are intimate beyond belief.

RÛMÎ

REMEMBRANCE

The Sufi aspires to remember God every moment of the day, with each and every breath. The dhikr, *the repetition of the name of God, is the fundamental practice of remembrance.*

There is a polish for everything that taketh away rust;
and the polish of the heart is the invocation of Allâh.

Hadîth

Say "Allâh!" then leave them to amuse themselves in
their folly.

Qur'ân

Remembrance makes people desire the journey:
it makes them into travellers.

Rûmî

Of all spiritual practices ... the *dhikr* is the practice most apt to free spiritual energy.... The advantage of the *dhikr* is that it is not restricted to any ritual hour; its only limitation is the personal capacity of the "student."

HENRY CORBIN

The breath that does not repeat the name of God is a wasted breath.

KABÎR

All the hundred-and-twenty-four-thousand prophets
were sent to preach one word. They bade the people say
"Allâh!" and devote themselves to Him. Those who heard
this word with the ear alone, let it go out by the other ear;
but those who heard it with their souls, imprinted it on
their souls and repeated it until it penetrated their hearts
and souls, and their whole being became this word. They
were made independent of the pronunciation of the word,
they were released from the sound and the letters. Having
understood the spiritual meaning of this word, they became
so absorbed in it that they were no more conscious of their
own non-existence.

ABÛ 'L-FADL MUHAMMAD IBN HASAN

Truth has been planted in the center of the heart as Allâh's trust, entrusted to you for safekeeping. It becomes manifest with true repentance and with true efforts. Its beauty shines on the surface when one remembers God and does the *dhikr*. At the first stage one recites the name of God with one's tongue; then when the heart becomes alive one recites inwardly with the heart.

'Abdu'l-Qâdir al-Gîlânî

Sahl said to one of his disciples: "Try to say continuously for one day: 'Allâh! Allâh! Allâh!' and do the same the next day and the day after, until it becomes a habit." Then he told him to repeat it at night also, until it became so familiar that the disciple repeated it even during his sleep. Then Sahl said, "Do not consciously repeat the Name any more, but let your whole faculties be engrossed in remembering Him!" The disciple did this until he became absorbed in the thought of God. One day, a piece of wood fell on his head and broke it. The drops of blood that dripped to the ground bore the legend, "Allâh! Allâh! Allâh!"

SAHL

A devotee was praying when Satan appeared to him
    and said:
"How long wilt thou cry 'O Allâh?' Be quiet for thou wilt
    get no answer."
The devotee hung his head in silence. After a while he
    had a vision of the prophet Khidr, who said to him,
        "Ah, why hast thou ceased to call on God?"
"Because the answer, 'Here I am,' came not," he replied.
Khidr said, "God hath ordered me to go to thee and say this:
'Was it not I that summoned thee to My service?
Did I not make thee busy with My name?
Thy calling "Allâh!" was My "Here I am,"
Thy yearning pain My messenger to thee.
Of all those tears and cries and supplications
I was the magnet, and I gave them wings.'"

Rûmî

I call to You.... No, it is You who calls me to Yourself.
How could I say, "It is You!" if you had not said to me,
"It is I?"

AL-HALLÂJ

I am the companion of him who remembers Me.

HADÎTH QUDSÎ

Whoever remembers Me in his heart, I remember him in
My heart, and whoever remembers Me to an assembly,
I remember him to an assembly better than his own.

HADÎTH QUDSÎ

Whoever recollects God in reality, forgets all else beside Him, because all the creatures recollect Him, as is witnessed by those who experience a revelation. I experienced this state from evening prayer until one third of the night was over, and I heard the voices of the creatures in the praise of God, with elevated voices so that I feared for my mind. I heard the fishes who said, "Praised be the King, the Most Holy, the Lord."

DHÛ-L-NÛN

Recollection is forgetting everything besides Him.

ABÛ SAʿÎD IBN ABÎ-L-KHAYR

God Most High hath said, "I give more to the one who is so occupied with My remembrance that he does not ask things of Me, than I give to the supplicants."

HADÎTH

Keep God, the Beloved, always in your heart. Let your prayer, *dhikr*, be the prayer of your heart.

'ABD'L-KHÂLIQ GHIJDUWÂNÎ

There are different levels of remembrance and each has different ways. Some are expressed outwardly with audible voice, some felt inwardly, silently, from the center of the heart. At the beginning one should declare in words what one remembers. Then stage by stage the remembrance spreads throughout one's being—descending to the heart then rising to the soul; then still further it reaches the realm of the secrets; further to the hidden; to the most hidden of the hidden. How far the remembrance penetrates, the level it reaches, depends solely on the extent to which Allâh in His bounty has guided one.

'ABDU'L-QÂDIR AL-GÎLÂNÎ

Dhikr is, in its reality, the progressive power of the Named on the heart, while the *dhikr* itself wears away and disappears.

AL-GHAZZÂLÎ

I make abundant remembrance of You not because
   I have forgotten You;
That is simply what flows from the tongue.

DHÛ-L-NÛN

Not a day passes but that the Exalted cries out, "O my
servant, you treat Me unjustly. I remember you, but You
forget Me. I invite you to Myself, but you go to others."

SAHL

One cannot taste the intimacy of remembrance without
having suffered the desolation of forgetfulness.

ABÛ 'UTHMÂN AL-HÎRÎ

There is a punishment for all things. The punishment for the mystic is to be cut off from His remembrance.

SUFYÂN ATH-THAWRÎ

When God wishes to befriend one of His servants, He opens for him the gate of His remembrance. When he experiences the sweetness of remembrance, He opens for him the gate of nearness. Then He raises him into the gatherings of His intimacy. Then He settles him upon the throne of unity. Then He lifts the veil from him and leads him into the abode of unicity and reveals for him the divine splendor and majesty. When his eyes fall upon the divine splendor and majesty, naught of himself remains. Thereupon His servant is entirely extinguished for a time. After this he comes under God's exalted protection, free from any pretensions of his self.

ABÛ SA'ÎD AL-KHARRÂZ

MEDITATION AND PRAYER

Meditation and prayer allow for the intimate communion of lover and Beloved and the inner experience of love's oneness.

Before He created them, He praised them; before they glorify Him, He gave them thanks.

AL-HALLÂJ

With the mountains, with the stone
Will I call Thee, Lord, o Lord!
With the birds in the early dawn
Will I call Thee, Lord, o Lord!

With the fishes in the sea,
With gazelles in deserts free,
With the mystic's call "O He!"
Will I call Thee, Lord, o Lord!

YÛNUS EMRE

O God! if I worship Thee in fear of Hell, burn me in
Hell; and if I worship Thee in hope of Paradise, exclude me
from Paradise; but if I worship Thee for Thine own sake,
withhold not Thine everlasting beauty.

RÂBI'A

You know that I am powerless to offer You a fitting
thanksgiving. Then come into me and give Yourself thanks.
This is the true prayer of thanksgiving! There is no other!

AL-HALLÂJ

And if I send Thee greetings, Thou art the greeting,
and if I speak, Thou art the prayer.

Maghribî

The eyes which regard God are also the eyes through
which He regards the world.

Traditional

"God is simple and loves simplicity," which is to say,
"Solitary, God loves only the solitary—One, He loves only
him who witnesses Him as One."

al-Hallâj

O my Lord, whatever share of this world Thou dost
bestow on me, bestow it on Thine enemies, and whatever
share of the next world Thou dost give to me, give it to
Thy friends—Thou art enough for me.

Râbi'a

What predominates in the heart of the mystic while he
is at prayer is his sense of the mystery of Him in Whose
Presence he stands and the might of Him Whom he seeks
and the love of Him Who favors him with familiar intercourse with Himself, and he is conscious of that until he
has finished praying and he departs with a face so changed
that his friends would not recognize him, because of the
awe that he feels at the Majesty of God.

Muhâsibî

O God, the night has passed and the day has dawned.
How I long to know if Thou hast accepted my prayers or
if Thou hast rejected them. Therefore console me for it
is Thine to console this state of mine. Thou hast given
me life and cared for me and Thine is the glory. If Thou
wantst to drive me from Thy door, yet I would not forsake
it, for the love that I bear in my heart towards Thee.

RÂBI'A

How is it that those people are most beautiful
     who pray at night?
Because they are alone with the All-Merciful
     who covers them with light from His light.

HASAN IBN 'ALÎ (GRANDSON OF THE PROPHET)

Worship God in such a way that you see Him. If you cannot do so be aware that He sees you.

AL-GHAZZÂLÎ

Become silent and go by the way of silence
  towards non-existence.
And when you become non-existent you will be
  all praise and all laud.

RÛMÎ

There are two types of silence: outer silence and silence of the heart and mind. The heart of one who trusts completely in God is silent, not demanding any means for living.

AL-QUSHAYRÎ

God is silence and is most easily reached in silence.

Bahâ' ad-dîn Naqshband

Silence for the ordinary people is with their tongues, silence for the mystics is with their hearts, and silence for lovers is with restraining the stray thoughts that come to their innermost beings.

Traditional

All this talk and turmoil and noise and movement
    is outside the veil;
inside the veil is silence and calm and peace.

Bâyezîd Bistâmî

The wise have inherited wisdom by means of silence and contemplation.

MAMSHADH AL-DINAWÂRÎ

Meditation is the chief possession of the mystic, that whereby the sincere and the God-fearing make progress on the journey to God.

MUHÂSIBÎ

I went to see Nûrî. I saw him sitting in meditation so motionless that not even one hair moved.

I asked, "From whom did you learn such deep meditation?"

"I learned it from a cat waiting by a mouse hole. The cat was much stiller than I."

AL-SHÎBLÎ

Bâyezîd Bistâmî, sitting at the feet of his teacher, was suddenly told, "Bâyezîd, fetch me that book from the window."

"The window? Which window?" asked Bâyezîd.

"Why," said the master, "you have been coming here all this time and did not see the window?"

"No," replied Bâyezîd. "What have I to do with the window? When I am before you I close my eyes to everything else. I have not come to stare about."

"Since that is so," said the teacher, "go back to Bestâm. Your work is completed."

BÂYEZÎD BISTÂMÎ

The best act of worship is watchfulness of the moments. That is, that the servant not look beyond his limit, and not contemplate anything other than his Lord, and not associate with anything other than his present moment.

ABÛ BAKR MUHAMMAD AL-WÂSITÎ

There was a ruler who had a servant for whom he cared more than his other servants; none of them was more valuable or more handsome than this one. The ruler was asked about this, so he wanted to make clear to them the superiority of this servant over others in service. One day he was riding with his entourage. In the distance was a snow-capped mountain. The ruler looked at that snow and bowed his head. The servant galloped off on his horse. The people did not know why he galloped off. In a short time he came back with some snow, and the ruler asked him, "How did you know I wanted snow?"

The servant replied, "Because you looked at it, and the look of the sultan comes only with firm intention."

So the ruler said, "I accord him special favor and honor, because for every person there is an occupation, and his occupation is observing my glances and watching my states of being attentively."

AL-QUSHAYRĪ

The best prayer is the one kindled by sorrow.

TRADITIONAL

God Most High hath brought forth creation and said,
"Entrust Me with your secrets. If you do not do this, then
look toward Me. If you do not do this, then listen to Me.
If you do not do this then wait at My door. If you do none
of this, at least tell me your needs."

SAHL

When a servant whom God loves prays to Him, God
says, "O Gabriel, delay answering the need of My servant,
for I love to hear his voice."

When a servant whom God dislikes prays to Him, God
says, "O Gabriel, answer My servant's needs, for I dislike
hearing his voice."

TRADITIONAL

Sâlih al-Murrî said, "Whoever is persistent in knocking at the door is on the verge of having it opened for him."

Râb'ia asked him, "How long are you going to say this? When was the door closed so that one had to ask to have it opened?"

SÂLIH AL-MURRÎ

The Children of Israel kept asking Moses: "Does God pray?" Moses kept quiet and did not answer. They urged him again and again. Finally God said to Moses, "You are My messenger; through you I communicate with My people. Tell them: God prays; and His prayer is, 'May My Mercy precede My Anger.'"

AL-HAKÎM AT-TIRMIDHÎ

SUFFERING AND SURRENDER

*Suffering is the pain of puri-
fication, cleansing the heart of
imperfections. Through suffering,
the lover learns to surrender to the
Beloved and become His slave.*

The self will not go in gladness and with caresses,
It must be chased with sorrow, drowned in tears.

PERSIAN POEM

Suffering is Himself, while good fortune comes
from Him.

AL-HALLÂJ

When does gold ore become gold? When it is put
through a process of fire. So the human being during the
training becomes as pure as gold through suffering. It is
the burning away of the dross. Suffering has a great
redeeming quality. As a drop of water falling on the desert
sand is sucked up immediately, so we must become
nothing and nowhere ... we must disappear.

Bʜᴀɪ Sᴀʜɪʙ

When God becomes friends with a man, He grants him
much distress and when He makes him His enemy, He
provides worldly goods in abundance.

Fᴜᴅᴀʏʟ ɪʙɴ ʻIʏâᴅ

O God! whatever punishment Thou mayst inflict upon
me, do not punish me with the humiliation of being veiled
from Thee.

ABÛ'L HASAN SARÎ AS-SAQATÎ

You imagined that you would accomplish this task
through your own strength, activity, and effort. This is the
wont that I have established: expend everything you have
in Our way. Then Our bounty will come to you. On this
endless road, We command you to travel with your own
feeble hands and feet. We know that you cannot traverse
this way with feet so feeble. Indeed, in a hundred thousand years you will not arrive at the first way station.
However, when you travel this road until your legs are
exhausted and you fall down flat, until you have no more
strength to move forward, then God's grace will take you
in its arms.

RÛMÎ

Sorrow and joy are your own attributes and whatever is your attribute is created, and the created has no access to the non-created.

IBN ʿATÂʾ

A bedouin was asked, "Do you acknowledge the Lord?"

He replied, "How could I not acknowledge Him who has sent me hunger, made me naked and impoverished, and caused me to wander from country to country?"

As he spoke thus, he entered a state of ecstasy.

ABÛ SAʿÎD IBN ABÎ-L-KHAYR

Do not chastise me for my devastation.
For the guide of love
Decreed the tavern of ruin for me
on the very first day.

HÂFIZ

God does not charge a soul with more than it can bear.

QUR'ÂN

I am with those whose hearts are broken for my sake.

HADÎTH QUDSÎ

Wherever there is a ruin, there is hope for treasure—
why do you not seek the treasure of God in the
    wasted heart?

RÛMÎ

The pain of love became the medicine for every heart,
The difficulty could never be solved without love.

'ATTÂR

Sweeter than this poison I did not see any drink,
Lovelier than this illness I did not see any health.

RÛMÎ

I burnt, and burnt and burnt.

RÛMÎ

Pain and happiness have the same shape in this world:
You may call the rose an open heart, or a broken heart.

DARD

Someone asked Junayd: "Slave of God who yet are free,
tell me how to reach a state of contentment." Junayd
replied: "When one has learned through love to accept."

AL-JUNAYD

When you die of surrender, only then you will
    live forever.
If you are put to death through surrender,
There is no such thing as death for you,
For you have died already.

PERSIAN POEM

I offer to Thee the only thing I have,
My capacity of being filled with Thee.

ANONYMOUS

Surrender is the most difficult thing in the world while
you are doing it and the easiest when it is done.

BHAI SAHIB

One builds the Self only with his full-accepted destiny.

AL-HALLÂJ

I want union with Him and He wants separation;
thus I leave what I want so that His wish comes true.

AL-GHAZZÂLÎ

Servitude is that you be His slave every instant, just as
He is your Lord every instant.

DHÛ-L-NÛN

Do you think I know what I'm doing?
That for one breath or half a breath
I belong to myself?

As much as a pen knows what it's writing,
or the ball can guess where it's going next.

Rûmî

I do not ask to see,
I do not ask to know,
I ask only to be used.

Anonymous

Sacrifice the self, otherwise don't be occupied with the foolish talk of the Sufis.

Abû Sa'îd ibn Abî-l-Khayr

POLISHING THE HEART

Sufis describe the heart as a mirror which the wayfarer polishes and polishes with aspiration and inner work, until no imperfection remains. Then the mirror of the heart can reflect the true light of the Beloved.

By means of the Divine Lights the heart becomes polished so that it shines like a polished mirror. When it becomes a mirror one can see in it the reflection of all existing things and the reflection of the Kingdom of God *as they really are.*

AL-HAKÎM AT-TIRMIDHÎ

Whether your lot be glory or disgrace, be pure of both hatred and love of self. Polish your mirror, and perhaps that sublime beauty from the regions of mystery will shine in your breast—just as it did for the prophets. And then, with your heart illuminated by that splendor, the secret of the Beloved will no longer be concealed from you.

JÂMÎ

For twelve years, I was the blacksmith of my soul. I
thrust my soul into the furnace of discipline and made it
hot in the flames of arduous endeavor, then I placed it
upon the anvil of reproach and hammered it with the
hammer of self-blame, till I had fashioned out of my soul a
mirror. For five years I was my own mirror, and I polished
that mirror with every manner of godly service and obedience. After that I gazed upon my own reflection for a year,
and I saw about my waist an infidel girdle of delusion and
coquetry and self-regard, because I relied upon my own
acts of obedience and approved of my own conduct.

BÂYEZÎD BISTÂMÎ

One has to work day and night,
to plough and to clean the field of the soul.

SANÂ'Î

If you find the mirror of the heart dull,
The rust has not been cleared from its face.

RÛMÎ

Struggle with all alien thoughts, be always mindful of
what you are doing and thinking. So that you may put
the imprint of your immortality on every passing incident
of your daily life.

'ABD'L-KHÂLIQ GHIJDUWÂNÎ

Purity of the heart is to will one thing.

TRADITIONAL

Sometimes He shows Himself in one way
Sometimes in the opposite way—the work
of religion is naught but bewilderment.

Rûmî

The Oneness of God, which is professed by the Sufis,
consists of: separating the created from the non-created,
going forth from one's native land, rejecting attachments,
and putting aside what one knows and what one does
not know, so that in place of all this there is the Real.

Abû Sa'îd ibn Abî-l-Khayr

I had hoped to get instructions in Yoga, expected wonderful teachings, but what the Teacher did was mainly to force me to face the darkness within myself, and it almost killed me. In other words, he made me "descend into hell," the cosmic drama enacted in every soul as soon as it dares lift its face to the Light.

IRINA TWEEDIE

When Majduddûn Baghdâdî entered the service of a sheikh, he was made to serve "at the place of ablution," i.e., to clean the latrines. His mother, a well-to-do lady physician, asked the master to exempt the tender boy from this work, and sent him twelve Turkish slaves to do the cleaning. But he replied, "You are a physician—if your son had an inflammation of the gall bladder, should I give the medicine to a Turkish slave instead of to him?"

JÂMÎ

Almighty God admitted me to His presence in two thousand stations, and in every station He offered me a kingdom, but I declined it. God said to me, "Bâyezîd, what do you desire?" I replied, "I desire not to desire."

Bâyezîd Bistâmî

For thirty years I sat watching over my heart. Then for ten years my heart watched over me. Now it is twenty years that I know nothing of my heart and my heart knows nothing of me.

al-Junayd

Strive to become the true human being:
one who knows love, one who knows pain.
Be full, be humble, be utterly silent,
be the bowl of wine passed from hand to hand.

AL-ANSÂRÎ

The meaning of noble character is that the harshness of
men does not affect you once you have become attentive
to God.

AL-HALLÂJ

If someone remarks "What an excellent man you are!" and this pleases you more than his saying, "What a bad man you are!" know that you are still a bad man.

SÛFYÂN ATH-THAWRÎ

Only that which cannot be lost in a shipwreck is yours.

AL-GHAZZÂLÎ

I will not serve God like a laborer, in expectation of
my wages.

RÂBI'A

All wisdom can be stated in two lines:

What's done for you—allow it to be done.
What you must do yourself—make sure you do it.

KHAWWÂS

Do to me what is worthy of Thee,
And not what is worthy of me.

SA'DÎ

Now the Lord is with them in every alteration,
Performing an unimaginable work in them hour
    after hour.
If they only knew! they would not withdraw from Him,
    not even for the space of a wink.
For He does not withdraw from them at any time....

AL-HALLÂJ

I met one of the young seekers in the desert under an acacia tree and asked him what made him sit there. He replied, "I am looking for something." Then I passed on and left him where he was. When I returned from the pilgrimage, I found he had moved to a spot closer to the tree. I asked, "Why are you sitting here?" He answered, "I found what I had been looking for in this place, so I stuck to it." I do not know which was more noble, his persistence in seeking his state or his perseverance in staying at the place where he attained his desire.

AL-JUNAYD

LIGHT UPON LIGHT

Sufis have given many mystical interpretations to passages in the Qur'ân. One of the most familiar and yet enigmatic Qur'ânic verses is the "verse of Light" (35) from Sura 24. Sufis have understood the inner meaning of this verse as a metaphor for the human heart, in which God's light resides and by which man is guided on his mystical journey.

God is the Light of the heavens and the earth,
His light may be compared to a niche
wherein is a lamp
the lamp in a glass
the glass as it were a glittering star
kindled from a Blessed tree
an olive that is neither of the East nor of the West
whose oil would almost shine forth
though no fire touches it.
Light upon light
God guides to His light whom He will.
God speaks in metaphors to me.
God has knowledge of all things.

QUR'ÂN (24:35)

God placed within the heart the knowledge of Him, and
so the heart became lit by God's Light. By this light He
gave the heart eyes to see. Then God spoke in a parable
and said, "Compared to a niche wherein is a lamp." The
lamp of the Divine Light is in the hearts of those who
believe in the Oneness of God.

AL-HAKÎM AT-TIRMIDHÎ

There are lights which ascend and lights which descend. The ascending lights are the lights of the heart; the descending lights are those of the Throne. The lower-self (the ego) is the veil between the Throne and the heart. When this veil is rent and a door opens in the heart, like springs towards like. Light rises toward light and light comes down upon light, "and it is light upon light."

Each time the heart sighs for the Throne, the Throne sighs for the heart, so they come to meet.... Each time a light rises up from you, a light comes down towards you, and each time a flame rises from you a corresponding flame comes down towards you.... If their energies are equal, they meet half-way.... But when the substance of light has grown in you, then this becomes a Whole in relation to what is of the same nature in Heaven: then it is the substance of light in Heaven which yearns for you and is attracted to your light, and it descends towards you. This is the secret of the mystical journey....

NAJM AL-DÎN KUBRÂ

Sorrow for His sake is a treasure in my heart. My heart is *light upon light*, a beautiful Mary with Jesus in the womb.

RÛMÎ

True ecstasy is the conjunction of light with light, when the soul of man meets the Divine Light.

'ABDU'L-QÂDIR AL-GÎLÂNÎ

The heart is the king and the limbs are its servants; each limb functions according to the will and command of the heart, yet the will of the heart comes from God. God nominates no one over the heart but Himself, and no one can see what the heart contains. God alone places in the heart and removes from the heart whatever He wills.... The heart is source and abode of God's Unity and object of God's observation....

God observes over the hearts for they are the containers of His most precious jewels and treasure stores of the true knowledge of Him.

AL-HAKÎM AT-TIRMIDHÎ

Dear friend, your heart is a polished mirror. You must wipe it clean of the veil of dust which has gathered upon it, because it is destined to reflect the light of divine secrets. When the light from *Allâh* (Who) *is the light of the heavens and the earth* begins to shine upon the regions of your heart, the lamp of the heart will be lit. The lamp of the heart is *in a glass, the glass as it were a brightly shining star....* Then within that heart, the lightning-shaft of divine revelations strikes. This lightning-shaft will emanate from the thunderclouds of meaning (heavenly Archetypes) *neither of the East nor of the West, lit from a blessed olive tree.* It will throw light upon the tree of discovery (or revelation), so pure, so transparent that it *sheds light though fire does not touch it.* Then the lamp of wisdom is lit by itself. How can it remain unlit when the light of Allâh's secrets shine over it?

It is not the stars that guide us but the divine light.... If only the lamp of divine secrets be kindled in your inner self the rest will come, either all at once or little by little.... The dark skies of unconsciousness will be lit by the divine presence and the peace and beauty of the full moon, which will rise from the horizon shedding *light upon light,* ever rising in the sky, passing through its appointed stages ... until it shines in glory in the center of the sky, dispersing the darkness of heedlessness.... Your night of unconsciousness will then see the brightness of the day.... Then you will see from the horizon of Divine Reason the sun of inner knowledge rising. It is your private sun, for you are the one *whom Allâh guides....* Finally, the knot will be untied ... and the veils will lift and the shells will shatter, revealing the fine beneath the coarse; the truth will uncover her face.

All this will begin when the mirror of your heart is cleansed. The light of Divine secrets will fall upon it if you are willing and ask for Him, from Him, with Him.

'Abdu'l-Qâdir al-Gîlânî

By means of the Divine Lights the heart becomes polished so that it shines like a polished mirror. When it becomes a mirror one can see in it the reflection of all existing things and the reflection of the Kingdom of God *as they really are.* When one sees the Glory and Majesty of God in His Realm then all the lights become one light and the chest becomes full with this shining light. He is like a man who observes his reflection in a mirror and sees in it at the same time the reflection of all that is before and behind him. Now when a ray of sun hits the mirror the whole house becomes flooded with light from the meeting of these two lights: the light of the sun-ray and the light of the mirror. Similarly the heart: when it is polished and shining it beholds the Realm of Divine Glory and the Divine Glory becomes revealed to it.

AL-HAKÎM AT-TIRMIDHÎ

O Light of light, Thou art veiled to Thy creatures and they do not attain to Thy light. O Light of light, Thy light illuminates the people of heaven and enlightens the people of earth. O Light of all light. Thy light is praised by all light.

PRAYER ATTRIBUTED TO MOHAMMED

THE LOVER AND THE BELOVED

For the Sufi the relationship with God is that of lover and Beloved. The lover travels a path from the pain of separation to the bliss of union. Yet the Beloved for whom he longs is eternally present within the heart.

He loves them and they love Him.

QUR'ÂN

In the whole of the universe there are only two, the lover and the Beloved. God loves His creation and the soul loves God. In order to be able to create, the One Being had to become two, and logically there had to be a difference between the two.... The creation was only possible because of the two opposites.

BHAI SAHIB

Man loves God, because of the affinity between the human soul and its Source, for it shares in the Divine nature and attributes, because through knowledge and love it can attain eternal life and itself become God-like.

al-Ghazzâlî

God is necessary to us in order that we may exist, while we are necessary to Him in order that He may be manifested to Himself. I give Him also life by knowing Him in my heart.

ibn 'Arabî

Not a single lover would seek union
if the Beloved were not seeking it.

Rûmî

In memory of the Beloved we drank a wine that made
us drunk before the creation of the vine.

Ibnu 'l-Fârid

O God, the stars are shining:
All eyes have closed in sleep;
The kings have locked their doors.
Each lover is alone, in secret, with the one he loves.
And I am here too: alone, hidden from all of them—
With You.

RÂBI'A

To one whom God has placed in the rank of His lovers,
He gives the vision of Himself, for He has sworn, saying,
"By My Glory, I will show him My Face and I will heal his
soul by the Vision of Myself."

MUHÂSIBÎ

I am nearer to you than yourself to yourself.

RŪMĪ

A caliph had a cousin whom he loved dearly. One day they were both sitting beside a well. The caliph's ring fell into the well. The girl took her own off and threw it into the well.

The caliph asked the girl, "Why did you do a thing like that?"

The girl replied, "I have known parting. Since a state of union and intimacy exists between us, I didn't want your ring to know the anxieties of separation. I gave my ring to be its companion."

ABŪ SAʿĪD IBN ABÎ-L-KHAYR

Zuleika let *every*thing be the name of Joseph,
    from celery seed to aloes-wood. She loved him
    so much, she concealed his name
in many different phrases, the inner meanings
    known only to her.
When she said, *The wax is softening near the fire,*
    she meant, My love is wanting me.
Or if she said, *Look the moon is up,* or
    The willow has new leaves,
or *The branches are trembling,* or *The coriander seeds
have caught fire,* or *The roses are opening,*
or *The king is in a good mood today,* or *Isn't that lucky,*
or *The furniture needs dusting,* or
The water carrier is here, or *It's almost daylight,* or
These vegetables are perfect, or *The bread needs more salt,*
or *The clouds seem to be moving against the wind,*
or *My head hurts,* or *My headache's better,*
anything she praises, it's Joseph's touch she means,
any complaint, it's his being away.
When she's hungry, it's for him. Thirsty, his name
    is a sherbet.
Cold, he's a fur. This is what the Friend can do
when one is in such love. Sensual people use the
    holy names
often, but they don't work for them.
The miracle Jesus did by being the name of God,
Zuleika felt in the name of *Joseph.*

RŪMĪ

129

If He hides His presence from you, it is because He is listening to you.

AL-HALLÂJ

My earth and My heaven containeth Me not, but the heart of My faithful servant containeth Me.

HADÎTH QUDSÎ

The love of God in its essence is really the illumination of the heart by joy because of its nearness to the Beloved, for love, in solitude, rises up triumphant and the heart of the lover is possessed by the sense of its fellowship with Him; and when solitude is combined with secret intercourse with the Beloved, the joy of that intercourse overwhelms the mind, so that it is no longer concerned with this world and what is therein.

MUHÂSIBÎ

Verily there are servants among my servants who love Me, and I love them, and they long for Me, and I long for them and they look at Me, and I look at them.... And their signs are that they preserve the shade at daytime as compassionately as a herdsman preserves his sheep, and they long for sunset as the bird longs for his nest at dusk, and when the night comes and the shadows become mixed and the beds are spread out and the bedsteads are put up and every lover is alone with his beloved, then they will stand on their feet and put their faces on the ground and will call Me with My word and will flatter Me with My graces, half crying and half weeping, half bewildered and half complaining, sometimes standing, sometimes sitting, sometimes kneeling, sometimes prostrating, and I see what they bear for My sake and I hear what they complain from My love.

AL-GHÂZZALÎ

The goblet of love is the lover's heart, not his reason or his sense perception. For the heart fluctuates from state to state, just as God—who is the Beloved—is *each day upon some task* (Qur'ân 55:29). So the lover undergoes constant variation of the Beloved in His acts.... Love has many diverse and mutually opposed properties. Hence nothing receives these properties except that which has the capacity to fluctuate along with love. This belongs only to the heart.

IBN ʿARABÎ

Al-Junayd was asked, "What makes the lover weep when he meets the Beloved?"

He answered, "This is only because of his great joy over Him and because of the ecstasy born of his great longing for Him. I have heard the story of two brothers who embraced after a long separation. One of them cried, "Ah, what longing!" The other responded, "Ah, what ecstasy.""

AL-JUNAYD

Real love does not diminish by the cruelty of the Beloved, nor does it grow by His grace, but is always the same.

YAHYÀ IBN MU'ÀDH AR-RÂZÎ

Verily, Almighty God has a wine for His friends, such that
when they drink of it, they become intoxicated, and once
they are intoxicated they become merry, and once they are
merry, they become purged, and once they are purged they
become melted down, and once they are melted down,
they become purified, and once they become purified they
arrive, and once they arrive they become united with the
Divine, and once they are united with the Divine there is
no distinction between them and their Beloved.

HADÎTH QUDSÎ

The being of the lover and Beloved are the same.

SHÂH NI'MATOLLÂH

Between the lover and the Beloved there must be no
veil. Thou thyself art thine own veil, Hâfiz—get out of
the way!

Hâfiz

The servant's love for God is a state too subtle for words.
This state brings him to glorify God and to try to gain His
pleasure. He has little patience in separation from Him,
feels an urgent longing for Him, finds no comfort in anything other than Him, and experiences intimacy in his heart
by making continual remembrance of Him. The servant's
love for God does not imply affection or enjoyment in the
human sense. Describing the lover as annihilated in the
Beloved is more fitting than describing him as having
enjoyment of Him.

al-Qushayrî

It is enough for the lover that he should make the One single.

AL-HALLÂJ

I came out from Bâyezîdness as a snake from its skin. Then I looked. I saw that lover, Beloved, and love are one because in that state of unification all can be one.

BÂYEZÎD BISTÂMÎ

Love means that the attributes of the lover are changed into those of the Beloved.

AL-JUNAYD

The true lover finds the light only if, like the candle,
he is his own fuel, consuming himself.

'ATTÂR

Not until *two* has been erased
will lover enjoy Union with Beloved.

AHMAD GHAZZÂLÎ

Everything is the Beloved, and the lover is a veil,
Living is the Beloved, and the lover is dead.

Rûmî

Dhû-l-Nûn met a woman on the seashore who revealed to him the mysteries of the path. He asked her, "What is the end of love?"

She answered, "O simpleton, love has no end."

He asked, "Why?"

"Because the Beloved has no end."

Dhû-l-Nûn

THE VALLEY OF LOVE

The power of love takes the Sufi wayfarer beyond the mind and the ego into the arena of the heart. Love is the fire that burns and transforms the lover, causing both bewilderment and intoxication, freeing the lover from everything but God.

In this valley, love is represented by fire, and reason by
smoke. When love comes, reason disappears. Reason
cannot live with the folly of love; love has nothing to do
with human reason. If you possessed inner sight, the atoms
of the visible world would be manifested to you. But if
you look at things with the eye of ordinary reason you will
never understand how necessary it is to love. Only a man
who has been tested and is free can feel this. He who
understands this journey should have a thousand hearts
so that he can sacrifice one at every moment.

'ATTÂR

I tell you the ways of love! Even though the head itself
must be given, why should you weep over it?

KABÎR

In every moment this love is more endless,
in every time people are more bewildered in it.

'ATTÂR

The heart alone knows what the substance of love is,
the eye of reason has no power to behold it.

ANONYMOUS

Love is a sweetness, but its inner reality is bewilderment.

ABÛ 'ALÎ AD-DAQQÂQ

I know nothing, I understand nothing, I am unaware of myself. I am in love, but with whom I do not know. My heart is at the same time both full and empty of love.

'ATTÂR

You may try a hundred things, but love alone will release you from yourself. So never flee from love—not even from love in an earthly guise—for it is a preparation for the supreme Truth.

JÂMÎ

Call me, and though Hell-fire lie between,
My love will make it easy to pass through the flames.

Abū Saʿīd ibn Abī-l-Khayr

sultan, saint, pickpocket;
love has everyone by the ear
dragging us to God by secret ways

I never knew
that God, too, desires us.

Rûmî

I planted a branch of desire for the people of love
And not one knew, before me, what desire was.
It sprouted branches, and sensual longing ripened
And left me with a bitter taste from the sweet fruits.
The desire of all the passionate lovers,
If they were to trace it, comes from that source.

IBN 'ATÂ'

Pure jewel! You have carried off my heart, without
telling me either your name or where you come from....
I have neither my own heart nor my heart's desire.

JÂMÎ

Oh who can cure my sickness? An outcast I have become. Family and home, where are they? No path leads back to them and none to my beloved. Broken are my name, my reputation, like glass smashed on a rock; broken is the drum which once spread the good news and my ears now only hear the drumbeat of separation.

Huntress, beautiful one, whose victim I am—limping, a willing target for your arrows. I follow obediently my beloved, who owns my soul. If she says "Get drunk," that is what I shall do. If she orders me to be mad, that is what I shall be.

NIZÂMÎ

Love is not to be learned from men; it is one of God's gifts and comes as a grace.

MA'RÛF AL-KARKHÎ

Love is the pre-eternal wine drunk by the elect on the
night of the Covenant.

AL-HALLÂJ

No one worships God by any act more pleasing to Him
than that of loving Him.

AL-HALLÂJ

A thing can be explained only by what is more subtle
than itself; there is nothing subtler than love: by what then
shall love be explained?

SUMNÛN

It is burning of the heart I want; this burning which is
  everything,
More precious than a worldly empire, because it calls
  God secretly, in the night.

RÛMÎ

The inner reality of love means that you give all of
yourself to the One until nothing remains of you for you.

ANONYMOUS

Love is a fire in the heart that burns up all but the
Beloved's wishes.

TRADITIONAL

He who loves does not think about his own life; to love truly, a man must forget about himself, be he ascetic or libertine. If your desires do not accord with your spirit, sacrifice them, and you will come to the end of your journey. If the body of desire obstructs the way, reject it; then fix your eyes in front and contemplate.

'ATTÂR

I would love to kiss you.
And the price of this kissing is your life.

Now my love is running towards my life shouting,
What a bargain, let's buy it.

RÛMÎ

Lovers do not reach the height of true love until one says to the other, "O Thou who art I."

ANONYMOUS

There is nothing good in love without death.

TRADITIONAL

Love means tearing down the veils and exposing the secrets.

Nûrî

The final end of love is to become bare. As long as love is in the beginning stage of its journey, the lover's nutriment is supplied by the form of the Beloved. However, once love reaches its final goal, it leaves behind every form. Just before this, the form of the Beloved appears in its perfection and falls as a hindrance between the lover and love. Thus the lover must spend all his effort to remove this veil.

Ahmad Ghazzâlî

Love means that all loves but love of the Beloved fall
away from the heart.

AL-JUNAYD

The beginning of love is search
But the end is rest.

ANONYMOUS

KNOWLEDGE OF GOD

A traditional Sufi saying states that "No one knows God but God." But in the hearts of His lovers He reveals His Divine mysteries.

True knowledge is what is unveiled in hearts.

TRADITIONAL

Knowledge acquired by external means will never reveal the Truth.

AL-GHAZZÂLÎ

God deposited within man knowledge of all things, then prevented him from perceiving what He had deposited within him.... This is one of the divine mysteries which reason denies and considers totally impossible. The nearness of this mystery to those ignorant of it is like God's nearness to His servant, as mentioned in His words, "We are nearer to him than you, but you do not see" (Qur'ân 56:85), and His words, "We are nearer to him than his jugular vein" (Qur'ân 50:16). In spite of this nearness, the person does not perceive and does not know ... *no one knows what is within himself until it is unveiled to him instant by instant.*

IBN 'ARABÎ

To know God is to love Him.

ANONYMOUS

If you would glimpse the beauty we revere
Look in your heart—its image will appear.
Make of your heart a looking-glass and see
Reflected there the Friend's nobility.

'ATTÂR

Love leads to knowledge of the Divine mysteries and
those who love abide in God and look to Him only, and He
is nearer to them than all else and to them is given a vision
of Him unveiled and they see Him with the eye of certainty.
Gnosis, truly, is a light which God casts into the heart.

'AMR IBN 'UTHMÂN AL-MAKKÎ

Insight consists of radiant lights in the heart, enabling mystics to carry secrets from one hidden realm to another, such that one may see things in the way that God displays them to him, so that he may speak about the innermost part of creation.

ABÛ BAKR MUHAMMAD AL-WÂSITÎ

The mystics are the treasure-houses of God: He deposits in them the knowledge of mysteries and information concerning wonderful things, and they speak of them with the tongue of eternity and interpret them with an interpretation which is everlasting.

ABÛ SA'ÎD AL-KHARRÂZ

The ecstasy of the Sufis is the sudden encounter of the
invisible with the invisible....

These are the realities which they find within their
innermost secret which emanates from the Divine Truth
without explanation.

ANONYMOUS

True knowledge of God is gained when the lover comes
in contact with the Beloved through secret communion
with Him.

ANONYMOUS

He who tastes, knows.

ANONYMOUS

When God wishes to conquer a heart, He entrusts it with secrets, which the heart then perceives and proclaims.

AL-Hallâj

Man is My secret and I am his secret. The inner knowledge of the spiritual essence is a secret of My secrets. Only I put this into the heart of My good servant, and none may know his state other than Me.

Hadîth

All that lies between the highest heaven and the earth does not amount to one atom compared with His power, and all existing knowledge cannot attain to one atom of the Lord's being.

Anonymous

He praises me, and I praise Him, and He worships me
    and I worship Him.
How can He be independent
When I help Him and I assist Him?
In my knowing Him, I create Him.

IBN ʿARABÎ

Who knows himself knows his Lord.

HADÎTH

In the ocean of life there is nothing more precious
    than to know oneself,
We have, therefore, chosen to revolve around ourselves
    like a whirlpool.

ANONYMOUS

There is nothing closer to you than yourself; if you don't know yourself, how will you know others? You might say, "I know myself," but you are mistaken!... The only thing you know about yourself is your physical appearance. The only thing you know about your *bâtin* (unconscious) is that when you are hungry you eat, when you are angry you fight, and when you are consumed with passion you make love. All animals are equal with you in this regard. You have to seek the truth within yourself.... What are you? Where have you come from and where are you going? What is your role in the world? Why have you been created? Where does your happiness lie? If you would like to know yourself, you should know that you are created by two things. One is your body and your outward appearance (*zâhir*) which you can see with your eyes. The other is your unconscious forces (*bâtin*). This is the part you cannot see but you can know it with your insight. The truth of your existence is in your *bâtin*. Everything else is a servant to your *bâtin*.

AL-GHAZZÂLÎ

When you know yourself, your "I-ness" vanishes and you know that you and God are one and the same.

IBN 'ARABÎ

The final and ultimate return of the mystics ... is that the Real is identical with them while they do not exist.... The mystic is known only through the fact that he brings opposites together, for all of him is the Real. Thus Abû Sa'îd al-Kharrâz was asked, "Through what have you known Allâh?" He replied, "Through the fact that He brings opposites together," for he had witnessed their coming together in himself.

IBN 'ARABÎ

Nothing sees God and dies, even as nothing sees God and lives, because His life is everlasting, and he who sees Him, remains in Him and is made everlasting.

ABÛ NU'AYM AL-ISFAHÂNÎ

When Bâyezîd was asked how old he was, he replied, "Four years."

They said, "How can that be?"

He answered, "I have been veiled from God by this world for seventy years, but I have seen Him during the last four years: the period in which one is veiled does not belong to one's life."

BÂYEZÎD BISTÂMÎ

When the mystic's spiritual eye is opened, his physical
eye is closed; he sees nothing but God.

ABÛ SULAYMÂN AD-DÂRÂNÎ

When the Beloved appears,
With what eye do I see Him?
With His eye, not with mine,
For none sees Him except Himself.

IBN 'ARABÎ

One who sees with the light of insight sees with the
light of God; the very substance of his knowledge comes
from God.

ABU SA'ÎD AL-KHARRÂZ

Whatever you imagine, God is the opposite of that.

Dhû-l-Nûn

Praise to God who hath given His creatures no way
of attaining to knowledge of Him except through their
inability to know Him.

Abû Bakr

Wheresoever you turn ...

One of the central mystical experiences is the oneness of God, the realization of the inner truth that "everything is He" (Hama ûst).

Wheresoever you turn, there is the face of Allâh.

Qur'ân

There is no God but He, everything perishes except His Face.

Qur'ân

When the mystery—of realizing that the mystic is one with the Divine—is revealed to you, you will understand that you are no other than God and that you have continued and will continue ... without when and without times. Then you will see all your actions to be His actions and all your attributes to be His attributes and your essence to be His essence, though you do not thereby become He or He you, in either the greatest or the least degree. "Everything is perishing save His Face," that is, there is nothing except His Face, "then, whithersoever you turn, there is the Face of God."

IBN 'ARABÎ

Rose and mirror and sun and moon—where are they?
Wherever we looked, there was always Thy face.

MÎR

Whether one is inclined to evil or good,
Whether one is an inmate of a cloister or a monk in a
    monastery
From the point of view of "form," everyone is other
    than He,
But from the point of view of reality everything is He
    and none other than He!

JÂMÎ

And in everything there is a witness for Him
that points to the fact that He is One.

ANONYMOUS

In the market, in the cloister—only God I saw.
In the valley and on the mountain—only God I saw.
Him I have seen beside me oft in tribulation;
In favor and in fortune—only God I saw.
In prayer and in fasting, in praise and contemplation,
In the religion of the Prophet—only God I saw.
Neither soul nor body, accident nor substance,
Qualities nor causes—only God I saw.
Like a candle I was melting in His fire;
Amidst the flames outflashing—only God I saw.
Myself with mine own eyes I saw most clearly,
But when I looked with God's eyes—only God I saw.
I passed away into nothingness, I vanished,
And lo, I was the All-living—only God I saw.

BÂBÂ KÛHÎ

The existence of the beggar is His existence and the
existence of the sick is His existence. Now when this
is admitted, it is acknowledged that this existence is His
existence and that the existence of all created things is His
existence, and when the secret of one atom of the atom is
clear, the secret of all created things, both outward and
inward, is clear, you do not see in this world or the next,
anything except God.

IBN ʿARABÎ

I was a hidden treasure, and I desired to be known,
so I created the world.

HADÎTH

Things lie hidden in their opposites, and but for the existence of opposites, the Opposer would have no manifestations.

AL-'ALAWÎ

He alone is the Observer, He alone is the Observed! There is none but He in the world of existence.

IBN 'ARABÎ

Sufism consists of keeping the heart from anything that is not He. But there is not anything not He.

ABÛ SA'ÎD IBN ABÎ-L-KHAYR

I am the Existent and the non-existent:
That which comes to nought and that which abides.
I am that which is felt and that which is imagined:
I am both the snake and the charmer.
I am the loosed and the bound:
I am that which is drunk and he who gives to drink.
I am the treasure and I am the poverty:
I am My creation and the Creator.

JÎLÎ

Whoever has fallen into the ocean of God's Oneness
grows thirstier every day. His thirst will never be appeased
because he has a thirst for truth and that is only quenched
by the Real.

YÛSUF IBN HUSAYN

Those who regard things as determined by God turn to
God in everything.

Nûrî

Abû Sa'îd was speaking before an assembly and he said,
"Today I am going to speak to you about astrology."
All the people listened to the Sheikh with keen interest,
wondering what he would say.
The Sheikh said, "Oh people, this year whatever God
wishes shall happen, just as last year everything that
happened was what God, He is exalted, wished."

Abû Sa'îd ibn Abî-l-Khayr

We and Thou are not separate from each other,
but we need Thee, whereas Thou doest not need us.

JÂMÎ

My servant ceases not to draw nigh unto Me by works
of devotion, until I love him, and when I love him I am
the eye by which he sees and the ear by which he hears.

HADITH QUDSÎ

He is now as He was. He is the One without oneness and the Single without singleness.... He is the very existence of the First and the very existence of the Last, and the very existence of the Outward and the very existence of the Inward. So there is no first nor last, nor outward nor inward, except Him, without these becoming Him or His becoming them.... By Himself He sees Himself, and by Himself He knows Himself. None sees Him other than He, and none perceives Him other than He. His veil, that is phenomenal existence, is a part of His oneness; nothing veils other than He. His veil is only the concealment of His existence in His oneness. None sees Him other than He, no sent Prophet, nor saint made perfect, nor angel brought nigh know Him. His Prophet is He, and His sending is He, and His word is He. He sent Himself with Himself to Himself.... There is no other and there is no existence other than He.

IBN ʿARABÎ

Sometimes we call Thee wine, sometimes goblet,
Sometimes we call Thee corn, and sometimes snare,
There is no letter save Thy name on the tablet
   of the world—
Now: by which name shall we call Thee?

Jâmî

In the name of Him Who has no name,
Who appears by whatever name you will call Him.

Dârâ Shikôh

God made this name—Allâh—a mirror for man, so that when he looks in it, he knows the true meaning of "God was and there was naught beside Him," and in that moment it is revealed to him that his speech is God's speech, his life God's life, his knowledge God's knowledge, his will God's will and his power God's power....

JĪLĪ

Annihilation of the Self

The Sufi seeks to "die before death," to transcend the ego and experience union with God. Transcending the ego is called fanâ *(annihilation), and is one of the most important stages on the path, leading to* baqâ *(everlasting life in God). In the depths of the heart the lover becomes lost in the formlessness of love. Merging with the infinite ocean of the Self, he experiences a complete nothingness that is absolute fulfilment.*

Between me and You there lingers an "it is I"
    which torments me.
Ah! lift through mercy this "it is I"
    from between us both!

AL-HALLÂJ

Go you, sweep out the dwelling-room of your heart,
prepare it to be the abode and home of the Beloved:
when you go out He will come in. Within you, when
you are free from self, He will show His Beauty.

MAHMÛD SHABISTARÎ

Oh Lord God! I do not want myself. Give me release
from myself.

ABÛ SA'ÎD IBN ABÎ-L-KHAYR

May God empty my very self
Of all except His own presence.

ANONYMOUS

The mystic is the knower without knowledge, without sight, without information, without apprehension, without description, without manifestation, and without veil. They (mystics) are not in themselves and if they are in themselves at all, they exist but in God. Their actions are held by God and their words are the words of God uttered by their tongues and their sight is the sight of God penetrated into their eyes.

DHÛ'L-NÛN

Oh Lord God, everyone has some wish, whereas I want to have no wish. And everyone has an "I," whereas I want to have no "I."

What I want is not to be me!

ABÛ'L-ABBÂS QÂSIM

A hundred spiritual masters have spoken concerning Sufism. The first said the same as the last. The modes of expression were different but the meaning was one: "Sufism is dropping all affectation."

And there is no affectation that comes before your own you-ness. The moment you become involved with your own self, you are cut off from Him.

ABÛ SA'ÎD IBN ABÎ-L-KHAYR

What you most want,
what you travel around wishing to find,
lose yourself as lovers lose themselves,
and you'll *be* that.

'ATTÂR

Know that when you learn to lose yourself, you will reach the Beloved. There is no other secret to be learned, and more than this is not known to me.

AL-ANSÂRÎ

An hour reflecting on one's own non-existence is better than a year of religious devotions with the thought that one exists.

ABÛ SA'ÎD IBN ABÎ-L-KHAYR

As I reached the stage of proximity to God, He said,
"What thou dost desire?" I replied, "I desire Thee."
He said, "As long as there remains even one particle
of Bâyezîdness in thee, that desire cannot be fulfilled."

BÂYEZÎD BISTÂMÎ

Kill me, O my faithful friends
for to kill me is to make me live;
My life is my death, and my death is my life.

AL-HALLÂJ

Thus it is that for your sake God protects you from yourself and causes you to pass by obliteration to eternal life, so that you achieve your desire and live eternally with Him.

AL-JUNAYD

First there must be action and knowledge, so that you realize that you know nothing and you are nobody. It is no easy thing to attain this realization. It doesn't come with teaching and instruction, nor can it be sewn on with a needle, or tied with a thread. This is a gift from God and a question of whom He bestows it on and whom He causes to experience it.

ABÛ SA'ÎD IBN ABÎ-L-KHAYR

Being wholly present in God, he is wholly lost to self.
And thus he is present before God, absent in himself;
absent and present at the same time. He is where he is
not and he is not where he is. Then after he has not been,
he is where he is (before creation). He is himself, after he
has not been truly himself. He is existent in himself and
existent in God after having been existent in God and
non-existent in himself. This is because he has left the
drunkenness of God's overwhelming and come to the
clarity of sobriety, and contemplation is once more re-
stored to him, so that he can put everything in its right
place and assess it correctly.

AL-JUNAYD

Twenty-two years I have been following in the footsteps
of at-Tirmidhî. He had no feature and now I have no
feature. Those who know will know and those who
understand will understand.

BAHÂ AD-DÎN NAQSHBAND

191

Who do you think I am? A drunkard? A love-sick fool, a
slave of my senses, made senseless by desire? Understand:
I have risen above all that, I am the King of Love in majesty.
My soul is purified from the darkness of lust, my longing
purged of low desire, my mind free from shame. I have
broken the teeming bazaar of the senses in my body.
Love is the essence of my being. Love is fire and I am
wood burnt by the flame. Love has moved in and adorned
the house, my self tied up its bundle and left. You imagine
that you see me, but I no longer exist: what remains is
the Beloved....

Nizâmî

I went from God to God, until He cried from me in
me, "O Thou I." Thus I attained the stage of annihilation
in God.

Bâyezîd Bistâmî

A certain person came to the Friend's door and knocked.
  "Who's there?"
  "It's me."
The Friend answered, "Go away. There's no place
for raw meat at this table."

The individual went wandering for a year.
Nothing but the fire of separation
can change hypocrisy and ego. The person returned
completely cooked,
walked up and down in front of the Friend's house,
gently knocked.
  "Who is it?"
"You."

"Please come in, my Self,
there's no place in this house for two."

RÛMÎ

One day in Nishapur, Abû Sa'id went to a mourning ceremony. The masters of ceremonies wanted to announce the Sheikh in accordance with their customs, and recite his titles. But when they saw the Sheikh they were at a loss, and asked his disciples: "What title should we apply to the Sheikh?"

The Sheikh saw their confusion and said to them, "Go inside and announce: 'Make way for No One, the son of No One!'"

ABÛ SA'ID IBN ABÎ-L-KHAYR

"The first time I entered the Holy House," stated Bâyezîd, "I saw the Holy House. The second time I entered it, I saw the Lord of the House. The third time I saw neither the House nor the Lord of the House."

By this Bâyezîd meant, "I became lost in God, so that I knew nothing. Had I seen at all, I would have seen God." Proof of this interpretation is given by the following anecdote:

A man came to the door of Bâyezîd and called out.

"Whom are you seeking?" asked Bâyezîd.

"Bâyezîd," replied the man.

"Poor wretch!" said Bâyezîd. "I have been seeking Bâyezîd for thirty years, and cannot find any trace or token of him."

Bâyezîd Bistâmî

The people of perfection have realized all stations and states and passed beyond these to the station above both majesty and beauty, so they have no attribute and no description. It was said to Bâyezîd, "How are you this morning?" He replied, "I have no morning and no evening; morning and evening belong to him who becomes delimited by attributes, and I have no attributes."

IBN ʿARABÎ

Neither am I aware of being a lover, nor of love,
Neither of my self, nor of the Beloved.

AHMAD GHAZZÂLÎ

Self-annihilation consists in this, that through the over-powering influence of the Very Being upon the inner man, there remains no consciousness of aught besides Him. Annihilation of annihilation consists in this, that there remains no consciousness even of that unconsciousness. It is evident that annihilation of annihilation is involved in annihilation.

JÂMÎ

Here is the candle extinguished and there the living light
　　of the Sun!
Mark the difference between the one and the other!

HÂFIZ

UNION

Travelling the path of love, the Sufi longs for union with the Beloved. Finally the heart reveals the Eternal Truth, that the lover and the Beloved are one.

I am He whom I love, and He whom I love is I.
We are two spirits dwelling in one body,
If thou seest me, thou seest Him;
And if thou seest Him, thou seest us both.

AL-HALLÂJ

Love has come and it flows like blood beneath my skin,
    through my veins.
It has emptied me of my self and filled me with
    the Beloved.
The Beloved has penetrated every cell of my body.
Of myself there remains only a name, everything else
    is Him.

RÛMÎ

When the lover is annihilated in Love his love becomes one with the Love of the Beloved, and then there is no bird and no wings, and his flight and love to God are by God's love to him.

Najm al-Dîn Kubrâ

I have embraced, with my whole being, all Your love, O my Holiness! You have manifested Yourself so much that it seems to me that there is only You in me!

I examine my heart amidst all that is not You.

I do not see any estrangement between them and me, and only familiarity between You and me!

al-Hallâj

Love has appeared from Eternity and will continue
till Eternity and none has been found in eighty thousand
worlds who could drink one drop of it until at last he is
united with God.

RÂBIʿA

Once He raised me up and caused me to stand before
Him and said to me, "O Bâyezîd, My creatures desire to
behold thee." I answered, "Adorn me with Thy Unity and
clothe me in Thy I-ness and raise me to Thy Oneness so
that when Thy creatures behold me they may say that they
behold Thee, and that only Thou mayst be there, not I."

BÂYEZÎD BISTÂMÎ

In the state of unification man perceives that all is He, and all is by Him, and all is His. What formerly was known by hearsay now becomes known intuitively as he contemplates the works of God. Then he entirely recognizes that he has not the right to say "I" or "mine."

ABÛ SA'ÎD IBN ABÎ-L-KHAYR

Glory be to me! How great is my majesty!

BÂYEZÎD BISTÂMÎ

Inside this robe there is only God.

ABÛ SAʿÎD IBN ABÎ-L-KHAYR

"Anâ 'l-ḥaqq" ("I am the Truth").

AL-HALLÂJ

His spirit is my spirit and my spirit is His spirit;
Let Him desire, and I desire—let me desire, He desires!

AL-HALLÂJ

There are moments of oneness with the Beloved, absolute ecstasy and bliss. That is nothingness. And this nothingness loves you, responds to you, fulfills you utterly and yet there is nothing there. You flow out like a river, without diminishing. This is the great mystical experience, the great ecstasy.

IRINA TWEEDIE

Union with God is separation from all else, and separation from all else is union with Him.

NÛRÎ

A boy stopped before the circle of Shiblî's followers and said, "Oh, Abû Bakr, remove me from myself and make me absent from myself and then give me back to myself, so that I am He and He is I and I am I and He is He."

ABÛ SA'ÎD IBN ABÎ-L-KHAYR

The one who has looked at the sun and then looks at himself, finds he is filled with nothing else but rays of the sun and exclaims, "I am the sun."

AL-HALLÂJ

I am God, there is no God beside me, so worship me.

BÂYEZÎD BISTÂMÎ

Whoever states that he has attained God, has not, whereas whoever states that he has been taken to God, has indeed attained union with God.

Abû'l-Hasan 'Ali al-Kharaqânî

When I love a devotee, I, the Lord, become his ear so that he hears through Me, I become his eye so that he sees through Me, I become his tongue so that he speaks through Me, and I become his hand so that he possesses through Me.

Dhû-l-Nûn

In God there is no duality. In that Presence "I" and "we" and "you" do not exist. "I" and "you" and "we" and "He" become one.... Since in the Unity there is no distinction, the Quest and the Way and the Seeker become one.

Mahmûd Shabistarî

Those who have attained union have nothing
but the inward eye and the divine lamp—
they have been delivered of signs and roads.

RÛMÎ

Nothing is better for a man than to be without anything—having no asceticism, no theory, no practice.
When he is without all, he is with all.

BÂYEZÎD BISTÂMÎ

The mystic is occupied neither with this world nor the
next: he is not concerned with any but his Lord. Because
he has died altogether to himself, he is completely
absorbed in the attainment of union with God.

'ATTÂR

It has been said that mystical poverty is the wearing
of the black raiment in the two universes. This saying
expresses the fact that the mystic is so totally absorbed
in God that he has no longer any existence of his own,
neither inwardly nor outwardly in this world and beyond;
he returns to his original essential poverty, and that is
poverty in the true sense. It is in this sense, when the
state of poverty has become total, that a mystic can say
that he is God....

LÂHÎJÎ

God created the hearts seven thousand years before the bodies and kept them in the station of proximity to Himself and He created the spirits seven thousand years before hearts and kept them in the garden of intimate fellowship with Himself, and the consciences—the innermost part— He created seven thousand years before the spirits and kept them in the degree of union with Himself. Then He imprisoned the conscience in the spirit and the spirit in the heart and the heart in the body. Then He tested them and sent them prophets, and then each began to seek his own station. The body occupied itself with prayer, the heart attained to love, the spirit arrived at proximity to its Lord, and the innermost part found rest and union in Him.

'AMR IBN 'UTHMÂN AL-MAKKÎ

How many words there were for you until when
I was able to meet you, I was made to forget them.

Anonymous

Then the pilgrim returns home, to the home of his origin
... that is the world of Allâh's proximity, that is where the
home of the inner pilgrim is, and that is where he returns.
This is all that can be explained, as much as the tongue
can say and the mind grasp. Beyond this no news can
be given, for beyond is the unperceivable, inconceivable,
indescribable.

'Abdu'l-Qâdir al-Gîlânî

BIOGRAPHICAL NOTES AND INDEX

'ABD'L-KHÂLIQ GHIJDUWÂNÎ (d. 1220). One of the foremost masters of the Naqshbandi Order; the spiritual teacher of Bahâ ad-dîn Naqshband and the master who introduced the "silent *dhikr.*" pp. 16, 24, 70, 104

'ABDU'L-QÂDIR AL-GÎLÂNÎ (d. 1166). The founder of the Qâdiriyya order, one of the earliest Sufi *tarîqas.* pp. 31, 65, 71, 116, 119, 211

ABÛ 'ALÎ AD-DAQQÂQ (d. 1015 or 1021). An important Sufi teacher from Nishapur who has become known mainly through the works of his devoted disciple Abu'l-Qâsim Qushayrî. pp. 9, 19, 24, 143

ABÛ BAKR (d. 634). The first Caliph, appointed by Muhammad as his successor; revered by the Naqshbandiyya as the first link in their *silsila* (chain of transmission). pg. 167

ABÛ NU'AYM AL-ISFAHÂNÎ (d. 1037). The author of a ten-volume compilation on Sufi masters entitled *Hilyat al-awliyâ'* (*The Ornament of the Friends*). pg. 165

ABÛ SA'ÎD AL-KHARRÂZ (d. 890 or 899). A disciple of Sarî as-Saqatî of Baghdad; one of the earliest Sufi authors. pp. 28, 73, 159, 166

ABÛ SAʿÎD IBN ABÎ-L-KHAYR (d. 1049). An illustrious master-poet from Nishapur (originally from the town of Mayhana in Khurasan), who had a tremendous influence on the Sufis of his time. pp. x, 3, 5, 7, 11, 18, 23, 28, 34, 35, 39, 42, 52, 57, 68, 93, 99, 105, 128, 145, 175, 177, 185, 188, 190, 194, 203, 204, 206

ABÛ ʿUTHMÂN AL-HÎRÎ (d. 910). One of the main masters of the School of Nishapur known as the *Malamatiyya*; the main disciple of Abû Hafs al-Haddâd and the teacher of Ismâʿîl ibn Nujayd al-Sulamî, who was the grandfather of the author of *Tabaqât al-Sûfiyya* (*The Generations of the Sufis*). pp. 27, 72

ABÛʾL-ʿABBÂS QÂSIM (b. AL-MAHDÎ SAYYÂRÎ). A tenth-century Sufi master from Merv (northeast Iran) who had many followers in his period. Founder of Sayyâriyya Sect, which does not exist anymore. pg. 186

ABÛ ʿL FADL MUHAMMAD IBN HASAN (d. 1023). Abû Saʿîd ibn Abî-l-Khayr's main Sufi teacher. pg. 64

ABÛʾL HASAN SARÎ AS-SAQATÎ (d. ca. 867). One of the early Sufis of Baghdad, a disciple of Maʿrûf al-Karkhî and the uncle and teacher of Junayd; has become a link in several of the Sufi "chains" (*silsila*). pp. 22, 92

AHMAD B. ʿASIM AL-ANTÂKÎ (d. ca. 835). Originally from Syria, though he may have lived in Baghdad where he became associated with Abû Hârith al-Muhâsibî; considered one of the early authors who wrote on mystical psychology. pg. 12

AHMAD GHAZZÂLÎ (d. 1126). The brother of the famous Abû Hâmid Ghazzâlî, whose successor he became as the head of the main religious academy in Baghdad; an inspiring Sufi author who wrote on music and ecstasy. pp. 138, 152, 196

ALAWÎ, AHMAD AL-' (d. 1934). A modern Sufi who founded a Sufi order in Algiers. pg. 175

'AMR IBN 'UTHMÂN AL-MAKKÎ (d. 909). A Baghdadi Sufi of the school of Junayd who objected to Hallâj's ecstatic outbursts. pp. 5, 158, 210

ANSÂRÎ, 'ABDULLÂH-I -AL (d. 1089). A Persian Sufi author from Herat (Afghanistan), famous for his *Manâzil al-sâ'irîn* (*The Spiritual Ranks of the Wayfarers*); was greatly inspired by Qushayrî and by Abû'l Hasan Kharâqânî. pp. 18, 19, 108, 188

'ATTÂR, FARÎDUDDÎN (d. 1220). One of the greatest Persian poets in the Sufi tradition, lived in Nishapur, wrote several great spiritual epics, the best known of which is *The Conference of the Birds*. Was killed during the Mongol invasion of Iran. pp. 17, 95, 138, 142, 143, 144, 150, 158, 187, 209

BÂBÂ KÛHÎ. A Persian Sufi poet. pg. 173

BAHÂ AD-DÎN NAQSHBAND (d. 1390). One of the most revered masters in the Sufi tradition; a follower in spirit of 'Abd'l-Khâliq Ghijduwânî, Naqshband re-instituted the "silent *dhikr*" and, consequently, the *tarîqa* of the Khwâjagân ("Masters") became known as the Naqshbandiyya. pp. 23, 45, 82, 191

BÂYEZÎD BISTÂMÎ (d. 874). An ecstatic Sufi from Iran who has become known for his intoxicated exclamations uttered in the state of "oneness," e.g., "Glory be to me! How great is my majesty!" pp. x, xii, 7, 19, 27, 49, 82, 84, 103, 107, 137, 165, 189, 192, 195, 202, 203, 206, 208

BHAI SAHIB (d. 1966). A Naqshbandi skeikh who lived in Kampur in northern India and who was the teacher of Irina Tweedie, as described by her in *Daughter of Fire.* pp. 36, 40, 41, 42, 91, 97, 124

BISHR IBN AL-HÂRITH AL-HÂFÎ (d. 841). One of the early Sufis of Khurasan who settled in Baghdad, where he became known for his piety and asceticism; *al-Hâfî* means "the barefooted," and reflects the type of asceticism which Bishr had adopted. pg. 10

CORBIN, HENRY (d. 1978). A French scholar and philosopher who had dedicated his life to the study of Muslim *wilâya* (or *walâya*) in Sufism and in Shi'ism. Among his best known books are *Creative Imagination in the Sufism of ibn 'Arabi* and *The Man of Light in Iranian Sufism.* pg. 63

DârÂ ShikÔh (d. 1659). A Muslim Indian prince and mystic who strove to reconcile Sufism and Hinduism; he wrote several treatises on Sufism and translated the Upanishads into Persian. It was the Latin translation of this Persian version which introduced the Upanishads into Europe at the turn of the nineteenth century. pg. 180

DârÂnî, AbÛ SulaymÂn ad- (d. 830). A Syrian Sufi with ascetic tendencies; known for his sayings favoring solitude, meditation, and celibacy. pg. 166

Dard, KhwÂja Mîr (d. 1785). An Urdu poet and mystic from Delhi, a descendant of BahÂ-ad-dîn Naqshband and a follower of the Naqshbandi Path through his father Muhammad NÂsir 'AndalÎb (d. 1758); his most famous work is his mystical autobiography 'Ilm al-KitÂb (*The Knowledge of the Book*). pg. 96

DhÛ-l-NÛn, ThaubÂn ibn IbrÂhim (d. 859). An early Sufi from Upper Egypt who had acquired an aura of great holiness in the Sufi tradition; known for his deep piety, wisdom, and love poetry. Because of his mystical theories he was persecuted by the Orthodox authorities, but his life was spared. pp. 2, 18, 31, 69, 72, 98, 139, 167, 186, 207

Fudayl ibn 'IyÂd (d. 803). A Sufi from Khurasan (northeast Iran) known for his asceticism, piety, and cheerlessness. pg. 91

GHAZZÂLÎ, ABÛ HÂMID AL- (d. 1111). One of the most celebrated Sufi writers and teachers. In his late forties he left a thriving career as a theologian in the great religious academy of Baghdad, went into solitude and wandering for several years in order to taste mystical truth through immediate experience. His greatest literary work is his *Ihyâ' 'Ulûm al-Dîn* (*The Revival of the Religious Sciences*) in which he strove to reconcile Sufism with Orthodox Islam. pp. xi, 4, 71, 81, 98, 109, 125, 132, 156, 163

HÂFIZ, MUHAMMAD SHAMSUDDÎN (d. 1389). From Shirâz (southeast Iran), one of the most celebrated Persian Sufi poets, he greatly refined Sufi love poetry; known for his "free spirit," nonconformity, and sense of humor. His poetry books have become oracles among Persian Sufis and non-Sufis alike. pp. 9, 35, 94, 136, 197

HALLÂJ, HUSAYN IBN MANSÛR AL- (d. 922). A Sufi from Baghdad who deviated from the teaching of "sober" mysticism taught by his teacher Junayd; expressed openly ecstatic mystical truths such as *anâ 'l Haqq* (I am Truth, I am God) which shook his contemporaries. Was accused of heresy and witchcraft and was crucified in front of cheering crowds in Baghdad. pp. x, 2, 17, 20, 21, 25, 68, 76, 77, 78, 90, 98, 108, 111, 130, 137, 148, 161, 184, 189, 200, 201, 204, 206

HASAN IBN 'ALÎ (d. ca. 669). The son of 'Alî ibn Abî Tâlib (the fourth Caliph and the revered leader of the Shi'ites);

through his mother Fâtima he is the grandson of the prophet Muhammad. pg. 80

Hujwîrî, 'Ali ibn 'Uthmân Data Ganj Bakhsh (d. 1071). A wandering Sufi from Afghanistan who wrote the earliest Sufi compilation in Persian; it is entitled *Kashf al-Mahjûb* (*The Unveiling of the Veiled*) and it contains many anecdotes and sayings of early Sufis, as well as of his contemporaries. pp. 3, 8, 30

ibn 'Arabî, Muhyî-d-dîn Muhammad (d. 1240). One of the greatest figures in Sufi history; Andalusian by origin, he traveled in the West and the East and has become known in Sufi circles as *ash-shaikh al-akbar* (the Great Sheikh). He wrote extensively, giving a philosophical framework to his deep mystical insights. His best known work is *Al-futûhât al-makiyya* (*Meccan Revelations*). Also known for his exquisite love poetry. pp. xi, xii, 37, 49, 125, 133, 157, 162, 164, 171, 174, 175, 179, 196

ibn 'Atâ', Abû'l-'Abbâs (d. 922). A close friend and disciple of Hallâj, the only one of his associates who had stood by him throughout his trial and execution; was himself executed in Baghdad because he would not denounce his friend and teacher. pp. 93, 146

Ibnu 'l-Fârid, 'Umar (d. 1235). An Egyptian Sufi poet who expressed his mystical longing in delicate and sophisticated love poetry. pg. 126

INAYAT KHAN (d. 1964). A Chistiyya sheikh who founded the Sufi Order of the West. pg. 37

JÂMÎ, MAULÂNÂ 'ABDU'R-RAHMÂN (d. 1492). One of the most eminent Persian poets and writers from Herat (Afghanistan) affiliated with the Naqshbandiyya Order. His best known work, *Nafahât al-'uns* (*The Breaths of Intimacy*), traces the Naqshbandi tradition and lineage. Through his literary work he introduced ibn 'Arabî's theosophy into the Naqshbandi lore. pp. 20, 59, 102, 106, 144, 146, 172, 178, 180, 197

JÎLÎ, 'ABDU'L KARÎM AL- (d. between 1408 and 1417). A Sufi author and philosopher; a descendant of 'Abd al-Qâdir Gîlanî; his main mystical teaching is described in his book *Al-Insân al-Kâmil* (*The Perfect Man*), a concept and theme inspired by ibn 'Arabî's works. pp. 41, 176, 181

JUNAYD, ABÛ'L-QÂSIM MUHAMMAD AL- (d. 910). The main Sufi teacher in Baghdad during the ninth century; many of the Sufis of his time clustered around him. He taught a type of mysticism which became known as "sobriety" (*sahw*) and was distinguished from the mysticism of "intoxication" (*sukr*) exemplified by Bistâmî and Hallâj. pp. x, 4, 5, 6, 12, 26, 59, 107, 111, 134, 137, 153, 190, 191

KABÎR, (d. ca. 1518). A mystical poet from India who combined Sufi ideas with Hindu imagery and vice versa. pp. 63, 142

KALÂBÂDHÎ, ABÛ BAKR MUHAMMAD (d. 990 or 994). The author of one of the earliest Sufi compilations, entitled *Kitâb al-ta'arruf li-madhhab ahl al-tasawwuf* (*Exploration of the Way of the Sufis*). pg. 45

KHARAQÂNÎ, ABÛ'L-HASAN 'ALÎ AL- (d. 1034). A most inspiring mystic from northern Iran, unlearned in the religious sciences of his age, but with unusual spiritual gifts; he did not have a master in the flesh but was initiated into the Sufi path by the spirit of Bayezîd Bistâmî. pp. 3, 34, 207

KHAWWÂS, IBRÂHÎM IBN AHMAD AL- (d. 904). An Iraqi Sufi known for his ascetic practices, poverty, and unconditional *tawakkul* (trust in God). pg. 110

LÂHÎJÎ, MUHAMMAD IBN YAHYÂ (d. ca. 1510). A Sufi author and commentator who has become known for his monumental commentary on Shabistarî's *Gulshan-i Râz* (*The Rose Garden of Mystery*), in which he combined Rûmî's lyricism with ibn 'Arabî's theosophy. pg. 209

MAGHRIBÎ, MUHAMMAD TABRÎZÎ (d. 1406). A Persian Sufi poet who had absorbed into his poetry the theosophical ideas of ibn 'Arabî on the "Oneness of Being" and "the Perfect Man," and who became instrumental in the distribution of these ideas. pp. 16, 55, 78

MA'RÛF AL-KARKHÎ (d. 815). An early mystic from Baghdad whose name is linked with Sarî al-Saqatî and al-Junayd, the masters of the ninth-century Baghdadi center. pp. 43, 147

Mîr Taqî Mîr (d. 1810). Urdu poet of the late eighteenth century. pg. 171

Muhâsibî, al-Hârith ibn Asad al- (d. 857). An early mystic from Baghdad, one of the first Sufi writers on questions related to mystical psychology. pp. 79, 83, 127, 131

Najm al-Dîn Kubrâ, Abû'l-Jannâb Ahmad (d. 1220). A great visionary in the Sufi tradition, a prolific writer from central Asia who had founded the Kubrawiyya order. Was killed during the Mongol invasion. pp. 115, 201

Nasafî, 'Azîz an- (d. 1282). Early exponent in the Persian language of ibn 'Arabî's mystical philosophy of "the Perfect Man" and the "Oneness of Being." pg. 30

Nizâmî, Ilyâs ibn Yûsuf (d. 1209). A Persian poet who preceded Rûmî in the tradition of Sufi love poetry. pp. 56, 147, 192

Nûrî, Abu'l-Husayn an- (d. 907). An eminent Sufi from Baghdad, affiliated with the school of Junayd. Because of his mystical poetry on Divine love he was accused of heresy, but was spared. Known for the rich imagery with which he described the "stations of the heart." pp. 7, 152, 177, 205

Nwyia, Paul (d. 1985). A Jesuit scholar from Beirut known for his studies on the formative period of Sufism, as well as for his work on the Shâdhiliyya Order and on

the Andalusian mystic ibn 'Abbâd of Ronda (d. 1390).
Was killed in the civil war in Lebanon. pg. 58

QUSHAYRÎ, ABÛ'L-QÂSIM 'ABDU'L-KARÎM AL- (d. 1074). One of
the great Sufi compilers of the eleventh century; an eminent
figure in his hometown Nishapur. His compilation entitled
al-Risâla fî 'ilm al-tasawwuf (*The Epistle on the Knowledge
of Sufism*) has become the classic textbook for Sufi novices.
pp. 50, 53, 81, 85, 136

RÂBI'A AL-'ADAWIYYA (d. 801). A female Sufi from Basra
famous for her devotional love for God and for her intoxi-
cating love poetry. A large part of the introduction of the
theme of Divine love into Islamic mysticism is attributed
to her. pp. 48, 55, 77, 79, 80, 110, 127, 202

RÛDHBÂRÎ, ABÛ 'ALÎ AHMAD AR- (d. 934). A Sufi from
Baghdad, follower of Junayd. Many of his fine sayings
have been compiled by Abû Nasr al-Sarrâj (d. 988) in his
Kitâb al-Luma' (*The Book of Scintillating Lights*). pg. 10

RÛMÎ, MAULÂNÂ JALÂLUDDÎN (d. 1273). A most illustrious
Sufi poet in the Persian language, from Konya (in modern
Turkey), his *Mathnawî* as well as his *Dîwân-i Shams-i
Tabrîz* have become inspirations to countless devotees
of "the Religion of Love." His mystical love poetry was
inspired by the spirit of his master Shamsuddîn Tabrîzî.
He founded the Mevleviyya Order known as The Whirling
Dervishes. pp. xi, 21, 26, 28, 29, 34, 36, 44, 45, 48, 49, 56,
58, 59, 62, 67, 81, 92, 95, 96, 99, 104, 105, 116, 126, 128,
129, 139, 145, 149, 150, 193, 200, 208

SA'DÎ, MUSLIHUDDÎN (d. 1292). A Persian poet from Shiraz, known for his didactic poetry as well as for his love poetry; his best known works are the *Gulistân* (*The Rose Garden*) and the *Bustân* (*The Orchard*). pp. 25, 29, 110

SAHL AT-TUSTARÎ, IBN 'ABDALLÂH (d. 896). One of the early Sufis of Iraq, known for his asceticism; exerted great influence on Junayd and his school. pp. 66, 72, 86

SANÂ'Î, ABÛ'L-MAJD MAJDÛD (d. 1131). A forerunner of Rûmî, from Ghazna (Afghanistan); one of the founders of Persian love poetry. pp. 58, 103

SHABISTARÎ, MAHMÛD ASH- (d. 1339). A Sufi poet from Tabriz, affiliated with the Kubrawiyya Order; his best known work, on which many commentaries have been written, is *Gulshan-i Râz* (*Rose Garden of Mystery*); it presents ibn 'Arabî's ideas in Persian mystical poetic form. pp. 184, 207

SHÂH NI'MATOLLÂH WALÎ (d. 1431). The founder of the Ni'matullâhi Sufi Order; born in Aleppo to a Sufi family, he travelled in Mecca, Shiraz, Transoxania, and central Asia where he had great followings; died in Mâhân, where his tomb still draws great crowds. pg. 135

SHIBLÎ, ABÛ BAKR IBN JAHDAR AL- (d. 945). An ecstatic Sufi from Baghdad, a disciple of Junayd and an associate of Hallâj; became known as a mystic whose intoxication resulted in "holy" madness; due to his madness he was spared of being accused of heresy and of the gallows. pp. 4, 53, 83

SUFYÂN ATH-THAWRÎ (d. 778). One of the early ascetics of Basra known for his piety, poverty, and lengthy meditations; an associate of Râbi'a al-'Adawiyya. pp. 73, 109

SUMNÛN IBN HAMZA AL-MUHIBB (d. after 900). A mystic from Baghdad, an associate of Junayd and his circle; known for his utterances on ecstatic love, hence his nickname *al-muhibb* ("the lover"). pp. 9, 148

TIRMIDHÎ, MUHAMMAD IBN 'ALÎ AL-HAKÎM AT- (d. ca. 907). An early mystic from Transoxania, known for his prolific writings on mystical psychology, the nature of the mystical path, and the description of the Friends of God (*awliyâ' allâh*). pp. 87, 102, 114, 117, 120

TWEEDIE, IRINA. The first Western woman to be trained according to the ancient Naqshbandi path of *Tyaga*, complete renunciation. Her teacher ordered her to keep a diary of her experiences, which became the book *Daughter of Fire*. pp. 40, 106, 205

WÂSITÎ, ABÛ BAKR MUHAMMAD AL- (d. after 932). A mystic from Baghdad, affiliated with the circle of Junayd; after the latter's death he moved to Khurasan and joined the Nishapuri school of the *Malâmatiyya*. pp. 84, 159

ACKNOWLEDGMENTS

For permission to use copyrighted material, the Editor gratefully wishes to acknowledge: Daniel Liebert, for permission to quote from *Rumi: Fragments, Ecstasies,* translated by Daniel Liebert; Khaniqahi-Nimatullahi Publications, for permission to quote from *Sufi Symbolism*, Volume One, Volume Two, and Volume Six, by Dr. Javad Nurbakhsh; Maypop Books, for permission to quote from *We are Three* translated by Coleman Barks; Mazda Publishers, for permission to quote from *The Secrets of God's Mystical Oneness* by Mohammad Ebn-e Monavvar, translated by John O'Kane: Meeramma Publications, for permission to quote from *Love's Fire* by Andrew Harvey; Mizan Press, for permission to quote from *Principles of Sufism* by al-Quahayri; Omega Press, for permission to quote from *The Hand of Poetry*; Pir Publications, for permission to quote from *Atom from the Sun of Knowledge* by Lex Hixon; SUNY Press, for permission to quote from *The Sufi Path of Love* by William Chittick; The Post-Apollo Press, for permission to quote from *Rumi and Sufism* by Eva de Vitray-Meyerovitch; Threshold Books, for permission to quote from *Open Secret* and *The Doorkeeper of the Heart* translated by Kabir Helminski; University of North Carolina Press, for permission to quote from *Mystical Dimensions of Islam* by Annemarie Schimmel, © 1978; Unwin Hyman Ltd., for permission to reproduce an extract taken from *Rumi Poet and Mystic* by R.A. Nicholson.

LLEWELLYN VAUGHAN-LEE, Ph.D., is the author of *The Lover and the Serpent: Dreamwork within a Sufi Tradition* (1990), *The Call and the Echo: Dreamwork and the Inner Journey* (1992), *The Bond with the Beloved: The Mystical Relationship of the Lover and the Beloved* (1993), and *In The Company of Friends* (1994). Born in 1953, he has followed the Naqshbandi Sufi Path since he was nineteen. In 1991 he moved from London to northern California, where he now lives with his wife and children. Dr. Vaughan-Lee lectures throughout the United States and Europe on Sufism, dreamwork, and Jungian psychology.

SARA SVIRI, Ph.D., has been a lecturer in Arabic and Islamic Studies at Hebrew University of Jerusalem and at Tel Aviv University. She is currently a lecturer at the Department of Hebrew and Jewish Studies, University College, London. Dr. Sviri also lectures on the psychology of Sufism at Birkbeck College, London, and is the author of numerous papers on Sufism and related subjects.

The Golden Sufi Center is a California religious non-profit corporation dedicated to making the teachings of the Naqshbandi Sufi path available to all seekers. For further information about the activities of the Center and Llewellyn Vaughan-Lee's lectures, or to order books and tapes, contact:

The Golden Sufi Center
P.O. Box 428
Inverness, California 94937

PHONE: (415) 663-8773
FAX: (415) 663-9128